health
nut

Health Nut

A Feel-Good Cookbook

JESS DAMUCK

Photographs by Linda Pugliese
and Roger Steffens

Abrams, New York

MAR

I'D R

Calif

SPRI

.dmv.c

Contents

Breakfast, Smoothies & Tonics

Beans & Legumes

Soups & Grain Bowls

Snacks, Starters, Sides & Salads

Plant-Forward Main Dishes

Desserts & Baked Goods

Staples, Dressings & Sauces

INTRO-
DUCTION

As much as I'm working on living in the present moment,
I do yearn for a way of life that was only possible in the 1970s.
My parents aren't full-fledged hippies, but they passed down
that longing—getting close but never fully realizing the dream
themselves. There were warped live recordings of Grateful
Dead tapes being played in family car rides when I was
growing up, I didn't know there were pancakes other than the
flat rubbery buckwheat variety, and my anxious mother came
to wear flowy clothes and patchouli after retiring—but true
crunchiness takes a balance of commitment and letting go that
was weighed down by the responsibilities of everyday life and
an unshakable agita that couldn't be masked by tie-dye.

Neurosis aside, the effort was there. My parents never gave me chocolate milk, instead chocolate rice milk boxes from Provisions in Sag Harbor were my treat before going to the playground. I didn't know that soda wasn't seltzer with a little bit of juice in it for much longer than you'd believe. We would travel to Vermont food co-ops and climb the postered stairway up to the Common Ground restaurant in Brattleboro to get hummus and sprout wraps every fall. I remember my dad doubting that Vermont life was a little bit slower than New York until, when shaking a bulk bin full of sesame chews, an employee interrupted and said, "Hey, man, you don't need to do that, it will come out, eventually."

My first restaurant job was being the juice girl every summer at Planet Bliss on Shelter Island. Beyond the orange sponge-painted walls and rustic lavender booths and through the swinging double kitchen doors, I

started blending up peach-raspberry-ginger smoothies and green juices when I was fourteen. Brunch shifts eventually evolved into dinners, and then to late nights behind the bar serving up cocktails made with freshly pressed citrus. Julie and Sebastian Bliss didn't just open a restaurant—it was a big, cozy living room, and they were the cool hippie parents of a bunch of weirdos. They kept us all full of really delicious organic, healthy food and threw the absolute wildest parties.

Sebastian's food was a true reflection of himself—influenced by travel to the best warm-water surfing around the world, granola enough, but always full of texture, flavor. It never took itself too seriously and couldn't have possibly had more love put into it, up until the last day the doors were open. The Mesclun Salad with Fried Tofu Croutons (page 187) was a staple, but it wasn't all straight-up health-food (e.g., the staff special, the Boozy Coffee Drink), though most of it was.

We wiped the tables down with parsley spray and a beloved black cat named Jezebel made her way through the restaurant every night. Local regulars, Hamptons celebrities, carnivores, and vegetarians all came to have their bodies and souls nourished. This balanced approach to food has always felt right to me, and you'll see my interpretation of it throughout this book.

At the Ross School in East Hampton, where I went to high school, regional, organic, seasonal, and sustainable food is part of the curriculum. Having access to produce that we grew in our school garden or neighboring farms, and learning about how to grow and purchase ingredients, where food and recipes came from, and why we eat them, and eating them in an environment where you actually wanted to hang out and talk to your friends and teachers remains one of the opportunities I am the most grateful for in this life, and it certainly instilled a way of eating that has stuck. At sixteen, I came to value yoga and eating a nutritious breakfast, and at thirty-five I can't believe how lucky I really was.

The good influences continued as the Sylvester Manor Farm began its CSA program down the street from our house. I wound up in Burlington, Vermont, for college, where organic local food was the rule at most restaurants in town. And then in New York, I lived one block away from Souen, the Japanese macrobiotic noodle haven, and Angelica Kitchen—a vegetarian mainstay where the Dragon Bowl Bargain, a rice bowl with soup and bread, was under $20 and could feed a twenty-something-year-old for more than a day. It would eventually be the Park Slope Food Co-op that kept me in New York longer than I had planned. I volunteered for monthly shifts arranging produce, which was an extremely satisfying escape from city life, and the low prices enticed me to schlep everything home on foot.

Attending the French Culinary Institute was a little conflicting for me. I started eating meat again to learn how to prepare it, and I ate more cream and butter than throughout the totality of my life—but the basics of creating flavor and how to treat vegetables certainly refined my craft.

As I worked with Martha Stewart for more than a decade, my cooking became a little less hippie and a little more elegant, but the principles were the same— the absolute freshest ingredients without any junk made for the most delicious food. Real food. When I started out as an intern for Martha's magazine, I was in charge of making her lunches, and this meant cooking dishes with hyper-local and seasonal ingredients, and

seemingly endless variety—it was never the same meal twice. And everything needed to feel "light, fresh, and truly delicious," which generally translated into lots of greens, nuts for texture, proteins, and healthy fats like avocado and wild salmon. These lunches were meals Martha could eat midday and feel satisfied but not sluggish (see page 129). Martha modeled a new version of what clean eating could look like to me, beginning with her favorite green juice in the morning (see recipe, page 77), and continuing to eat mostly vegetables the rest of the day. When she brought in fresh eggs or big bundles of asparagus and greens from her garden, this was even more inspiring. When I worked for Martha's *Everyday Food* magazine as an editor, the focus was coming up with innovative new recipes for nutritious food made from ingredients you could find at any grocery store, which was sometimes really challenging, but helped me rein in my use of esoteric, hard-to-find ingredients and tendency to create recipes that employed every pot and pan in the kitchen—all invaluable lessons for a recipe developer. It should be noted that my former boss, *Everyday Food* editor-in-chief Sarah Carey's little face can be found within the "A" of *FEAST: A Cookbook by the True Light Beavers*, one of the most incredible examples of commune cookbooks from the early seventies. Sarah, who grew up as part of this counterculture commune, remains one of the best resources for info on domes, TVP, and chicken plucking.

Salad Freak, my first book, is a collection of recipes that pushes the definition of what a salad can be, inspired by my time at Martha Stewart. Focusing on creating delicious, exciting salads is how I first learned to eat in a sustainable way, but there are healthy feel-good foods that I love that fall completely outside the salad category. Granolas, grains, and eggs for breakfast are always on rotation in my house. Sometimes a warm savory pasta dish or a big bowl of soup just hits right (and is great served alongside a salad for a heartier meal). And while there are some new salads in the pages that follow, most of the recipes are veg-heavy main dishes, satisfying enough for a complete meal. But you can absolutely use my books together to add more variety and create really beautiful, colorful, healthy meals, full of textures and flavors.

It is no surprise that while writing *Salad Freak*, I ended up in Los Angeles, where health food as we know it today began. The pull of the sun-drenched city where everyone seems to glow a bit brighter has always been strong. Being able to grow my own ingredients has taken things to a whole new dimension. We may not have traveled back to the time of hippies and communes, but slowly, my partner Ben and I are creating the closest thing we can to a community built around a certain kind of vibe and really good good-for-you food. This book is my collection of just that. Inspired by the incredible vintage books I keep on my shelves (*The New Farm Vegetarian Cookbook*, *Moosewood*, *Enchanted Broccoli Forest*, *Spiritual Nutrition*, *Laurel's Kitchen*, *Kripalu Kitchen*, among others), my take on healthy cooking is fresh, colorful, beautiful, and not-too-difficult. Organic, once hard-to-find ingredients are more accessible than ever. While it is very sad to see many mom 'n' pop independent health food stores closing their doors because of big-box competition, through CSAs, nationwide stores such as Whole Foods, "ugly produce" delivery services, and most farmers' markets accepting SNAP dollars, with a little extra effort these ingredients are available in most neighborhoods. And don't forget, while some of these items may be more expensive, it really is an investment in yourself and in your health. There is no doubt you'll feel better eating more vegetables and less processed food, and it really doesn't have to be bland or boring. Or tofu. There really isn't that much tofu in this book.

ABOUT THIS BOOK

I am not a nutritionist. I am not a wellness influencer. I am just a classically French–trained chef who has a nostalgia for the sticky shelved health food stores that are becoming increasingly hard to find. I am someone who worked with Martha Stewart for a long time, loves to garden, is obsessed with produce, and has a huge collection of cookbooks from the seventies. In this book you will find a lot of plant-forward meals, and not a lot of refined sugar—but you will also find a little butter, some all-purpose flour, an almost unreasonable number of dates, and lots of nuts, olive oil, coconut oil, and other "good fats." Is it truly health food? Who's to say—but it is real food. This is a collection of the food that I feel good eating, but don't feel like I'm depriving myself of anything. It's food I like to feed the people around my table. It also looks beautiful and tastes great.

I have noted substitutions wherever I've thought of them for harder-to-find or seasonal ingredients, but I also encourage you to make tweaks to the recipes based on your own intuition. Use the charts to refine your methods for cooking beans (page 271) and grains (page 268) and to get creative when making bowls (page 277). Most of the recipes are naturally vegan or gluten-free, and if not, you can swap in 1-to-1 gluten-free flour, gluten-free bread crumbs, vegan butter, vegan egg replacer, etc.

I hope this book will scratch the itch when you need to nourish yourself and replenish yourself (and others). I hope you can find some inspiration when you're feeling a lack, a comfort in knowing there is a place you can turn. This cookbook is very much a reflection of my home, and I hope it becomes a big part of your home too.

For Every Body

I wish I could say I'm an expert on this topic, as many wellness people are or claim to be, but my struggles with my own self-image continue, and my own judgments have even been heightened at times while working on this book. I find most books on this topic, and motivational Instagram posts, can be broad and unhelpful, and just tend to put more pressure on me, as a perfectionist, to "fix" myself in some way. Personally, most body-positivity media also does not land. Consistently, most "healthy" cookbooks or websites I open seem to be perpetuating a lot of restrictive diets and "aspirational" lifestyles, and I really have tried to check myself while making this book to make it . . . not that.

Growing up, I was taught how to physically take care of myself, but I can't remember ever being shown how to love and appreciate my body—to respect it, or to even be amazed by it! I feel so grateful I grew up pre–social media, but even without it, it was hard enough. Bullies never go away, and little jabs, teasing, and full-on trolling can be internalized and haunt you your whole life. Having a family that puts a lot of focus on your appearance, good or bad, can be difficult too. Seeing billboards, movies, and magazines . . . even now, I struggle with being my own harshest critic, and find it impossible to ignore the pressure from constant reminders of society's beauty standards, especially now that I live in Los Angeles.

Food has its role in all this as well, in both healthy and unhealthy ways. Sometimes focusing on healthy eating can become obsessive, leading to guilt, restriction, and judgment of oneself or others. But eating well and preparing nutritious meals for yourself and those around you is also a powerful tool to feeling and looking healthier, and can give you a lot more energy, and really help to show yourself some love. Building more confidence in the kitchen is a skill set that radiates into your life. For me it's a bit of a crutch sometimes, but it's something I have always really taken pride in, and I feel so good when I can share it, or even just make myself something instead of ordering in.

I have worked hard to learn to love myself, but it's an ongoing process. I wish it were as easy as taking baths when you're tired or replacing your morning latte with a matcha or doing Pilates a couple of times a week. Really, the only advice I can give while remaining completely authentic is to try to surround yourself with people who make you feel good. There will always be someone or something around to trigger your insecurities, but finding one or two people who lift you up, just accept you as you are, who will be open and honest with you, to push you sometimes, and who know how to really make you laugh—that's what really grounds me and helps me grow. And if you're anything like me, just remember to be a *little* easier on yourself—cut yourself some slack. Yes, get some movement during your day that feels good, and yes, try meditation and breathwork and therapy, but more than anything, if you're feeling bad about yourself or in your body, just try to be a *little* more kind.

When I was growing up, there was a character who walked around my small town, the sort of guy you couldn't miss, and you ran into everywhere. Whenever you parted ways with him, he'd always say the same thing: "Don't change, you're beautiful." You know what? Maybe just start saying that. I think we could all use the reminder.

THE
FAMILY ACID

The first time we spoke, I called Roger Steffens on his landline, and his booming radio announcer voice struck me. "I met my wife, Mary, while on LSD under a total eclipse of the moon in a pygmy forest in Mendocino in 1975, and we've been together ever since," was how he started the conversation. We became fast friends.

Roger has been documenting California counterculture since 1968, when he returned from service in Vietnam (where his interest in photography began) and headed west. I have always been a huge fan of his work, and I didn't think a book that was inspired by 1970s California health food could or should exist without his well-known psychedelic double-exposure photography. Roger has a collection of more than 100,000 film images his son Devon and daughter Kate have helped digitize, creating "The Family Acid," which can be enjoyed on Instagram and in their many books. And I was ecstatic when he agreed to shoot original images at my home for this book, which you'll see sprinkled throughout these pages.

Roger also is the keeper and collector of the Reggae Archives, has the world's largest collection of Bob Marley and reggae ephemera and records, and signs off every conversation saying "One love." We spent a whole afternoon viewing the lower level of his home and learning more than ever before about reggae, and how he introduced Paul Simon to Ladysmith Black Mambazo (right before they started working on *Graceland*), and how Keith Richards stood in the very spot we were standing and looked at a photo of the clouds on the stairs and clearly saw Haile Selassie in the parting of the sky.

Getting to know Roger and Mary was a little bit like Ben and I having the opportunity to look into a crystal ball of the future, I hope. At eighty-one, Roger climbed up my steep driveway and under and through my cactus garden and showed tireless inspiration while shooting every bit of nature and every one of my friends' faces late into the night, while telling stories the whole time. It was the kind of chaotic creativity there is no use trying to contain or control, which felt very familiar in this house.

THE NEW HIPPIE KITCHEN

When it comes to the word *hippie* in regards to food, I think of co-op bulk food bins, jars of sprouts, and carob energy chunks. But I've come to embrace that word to mean real food, food that's good for you. Lots of fresh stuff, mostly organic, and incredibly earthy. These foods have crunch, tang, brightness, sweetness; they hit all the notes but blow your taste buds open, naturally, if that makes sense. It's a subtle taste explosion that is about enhancing the ingredients.

These days, my pantry feels more out of control than ever. It spills onto my counter and plunges deeper into the abyss of the cabinet above the refrigerator. So many vinegars, so many alternative flours. I wish I could just keep it simple. The good news is that you can! Here are some basics, and some health food must-haves.

Among a few other essential kitchen tools that I'll describe here, I do recommend buying a bunch of large canning jars with tight-fitting lids, or clear plastic stackable storage containers to store items from bulk bin shopping, and to keep ingredients fresh and organized.

Oils and Vinegars

These are the oils and vinegars you will need to make everything in this book. There are many other amazing vinegars in the world, but these are a great place to start.

Apple Cider Vinegar: I always buy Bragg's. It's great for vinaigrettes and flavoring sauces, great as a base to make infused vinegars, and great as a morning tonic in a big glass of water.

Balsamic Vinegar: I don't use balsamic vinegar that often, so I invest in a good one from Modena, which can range in price from about $15 to over $100. Think of it as a bottle of wine—somewhere around the $30 mark usually delivers a very good-quality balsamic that you'll want to drizzle on everything.

Coconut Oil: I use Dr. Bronner's Whole-Kernel Unrefined Virgin Coconut Oil. This oil has a smoke point of about 350°F (175°C) and is suitable for baking, sauteing at medium-high heat, and slathering all over your body or adding to bathwater. Refined coconut oil has been heated to remove impurities, and this process gives it a higher smoke point of about 450°F (230°C).

Extra-Virgin Olive Oil: The most important things to look for in an olive oil are that (a) it is extra-virgin, (b) it is single origin, and (c) it is stored in a container that blocks light—tins, plastic, or green glass is best. I usually keep a strong young olive oil for drizzling as well. My favorite olive oil for cooking is Graza— it is mild and fruity and adds flavor without being overpowering.

Ghee: This is a clarified butter, which has been heated and strained to remove all milk solids. This gives ghee a higher smoke point and a rich, nutty flavor and makes it suitable for those who are lactose sensitive. Ghee also contains butrate, a fatty acid that has been proven to reduce inflammation. It is used in ayurvedic cooking because of this and numerous other health-boosting properties.

Neutral Oils: Refined avocado, peanut, safflower, sunflower, and grapeseed are the neutral oils I like to cook with. They have high smoke points and are great for frying, or for cooking when you don't want the flavor of a stronger-tasting oil, like olive oil.

Rice Vinegar: Clean, bright, not overwhelming, it's perfect for seasoning rice and making light vinaigrettes; or use a little splash to brighten things up.

Sherry Vinegar: Super punchy! Its complex flavor gives that *je ne sais quoi* to simple vinaigrettes. Look for something aged for an even more interesting profile.

Toasted Sesame Oil: Make sure to keep this in the fridge! This is a finishing oil. It is full of flavor but should not be used for cooking.

Umeboshi (Ume Plum) Vinegar: This vinegar is the pickling liquid from umeboshi (pickled plums). It has a beautiful pink color and a sour, tangy, kind of funky flavor that my friend Lauryn describes as "fish sauce adjacent."

The Spice Trip

There is a big misconception that health food has to be bland or boring, but that's really only if you're following a macrobiotic diet or are trying to get off the flavor trip in favor of spiritual goals. Here are some of my favorite things that can add a lot of flavor to your cooking. Make sure when you are buying dried spices to get them from a high-quality source. It's tempting to save money and buy in bulk, but most spices begin to lose flavor after about a year. Diaspora Spice Co, Burlap and Barrel, and SOS Chef are my favorite sources for incredible spices. Toiro and the Japanese Pantry are great online retailers of the best-quality Japanese ingredients.

Canned Cherry Tomatoes: I love the taste of these sweet and tangy canned cherry tomatoes. I usually buy the Mutti brand, but Cento, Colavita, and several other brands are available as well. Italian markets also will have them.

Cocoa Powder: I use Valrhona 100-percent cocoa powder. It is unsweetened, incredibly rich, and as far as I know the best-tasting and highest-quality cocoa powder available. Cocoa powder is full of antioxidants and other healthy compounds.

Coconut Milk: The milk is the liquid that is extracted from the meat of a coconut. I really like to treat myself to the Chaokoh brand from Thai grocery stores. I stock up on it; there is nothing better.

Coconut Cream: Made from skimming the top layer off coconut milk, it is creamier, richer, and has a stronger coconut flavor than coconut milk.

Dried Chiles: Masienda and Boonville Barn Collective have an amazing selection of really fresh dried chiles available online, but Mexican grocery stores are another great source.

Furikake: This Japanese condiment, which is great sprinkled on cooked rice, vegetables, or fish, is an incredibly delicious, flavorful mixture usually containing sesame seeds, seaweed, salt, and sometimes bonito or other dried fish or seasonings.

Gomasio: A staple of macrobiotic cooking, gomasio is ground sesame-seed salt. The oil of toasted ground sesame seed enhances the flavor of the salt and rounds out the flavor.

Harissa Paste: A spicy North African pepper-based paste adds the perfect kick to veggie dishes, eggs, sauces, and more.

Liquid Aminos: It's a lot like soy sauce, but it's not derived from soy and it's gluten free!

Mushroom Powder: Sometimes referred to as "umami powder," this is essentially dehydrated mushrooms that are finely ground. You can make your own with fresh mushrooms, buy already dried mushrooms, or find mushroom powder at most health food stores or even Trader Joe's!

Nutritional Yeast:
I recently heard it's also called Nooch. These inactive flakes of brewer's yeast contain a lot of vitamin B12 (which is great if you're veg or vegan) and naturally occurring glutamic acid, aka the same thing that gives Parmesan cheese that amazing umami flavor. So it's great as a substitute for cheese in sauces and as a seasoning all on its own. If you need an entry point, just put it on some popcorn (see page 145).

Ponzu Sauce: A Japanese citrus-based tangy dipping sauce that is a mix of citrus juice (usually yuzu), vinegar, soy sauce, sugar, mirin, and dashi (bonito and kombu). Make it from scratch if you have a stocked Japanese pantry, but store-bought options are great.

Seaweed: Available in many forms, dried seaweed such as nori and wakame are available in most health food stores, Whole Foods, and conventional markets as well. Dulse flakes and kelp seasoning are great to use as low-salt seasonings.

Smoked Soy Sauce: This one is expensive but a little goes a long way, and in vegetarian and vegan cooking it's an absolute game-changer. Just a little drop of this packs the boldest smoky umami flavor. It's available online from several retailers—I love the Yugeta Shoyu brand.

Tahini: The truth is, this could have been a whole book just about tahini. This sesame paste is it. I love the Soom brand.

Tamari: Gluten-free soy sauce that has a deeper, richer, more umami flavor.

Togarashi: A spicy Japanese condiment, also known as Shichimi Togarashi. *Shichi* means *seven*, which is the usual number of spices in this flavorful blend that typically includes red chiles, Sichuan peppercorns, dried citrus peel, black sesame seeds, white sesame seeds, ground ginger, poppy seeds, and nori.

Sweet Stuff

Agave: Made from the agave plant, agave nectar is refined but has a lower glycemic index than sugar (thus raises your blood sugar a bit more slowly). I only use it to sweeten drinks, because it mixes easily into cold liquids.

Cane Sugar: Organic cane sugar is a bit better for you, and much more sustainable and less processed, than conventional sugar.

Carob: This dairy-free chocolate alternative (that doesn't really taste like chocolate) also contains fiber, antioxidants, low amounts of sugar, no caffeine, and no gluten. It has its own sweet, nutty, delicious flavor.

Dates and Date Syrup: This book uses an unreasonable number of dates, but they really are nature's candy and offer so much natural sweetness and other nutrients, along with a deep caramel flavor. Go for the super-soft Medjool variety: I love Rancho Meladuco California Dates and Joolies, which are available nationwide.

Honey: Honey tastes sweeter than sugar, so you can often use less, and it contains small amounts of vitamins and minerals. There are more than three hundred varieties of honey made in the United States.

Maple Syrup: Lower on the glycemic index than sugar, maple syrup is made of tree sap and is less processed than other sugars.

Rice, Grains, and Flours

Brown Rice: A central part of macrobiotic cooking, brown rice still contains the bran and germ covering of the rice grain, making it more nutritious than white rice, and giving it a chewy texture and nutty flavor.

Buckwheat: I hate to play favorites, but I CRAVE buckwheat. Contrary to its name, it's not wheat at all, but a pseudo-cereal. This flour has an extremely nutty flavor and is completely gluten free. It comes in both light and dark (unhulled) forms, and I prefer the latter, which is almost black and a little grittier but has a really strong flavor. This is what soba noodles are made from! Buckwheat groats (kasha) are another way to enjoy buckwheat in its grain form.

Masa Harina: This is a flavorful flour made from nixtamalized corn. The corn is soaked in lime water to soften the kernel, so it is easier to grind into a flour to make tortillas, but it also makes it easier to digest and makes some of the nutrients more bioavailable. I prefer it over corn flour or cornmeal, because it has a stronger corn flavor. I do really feel like it's worth it. Also, it's less likely to be contaminated with wheat—good to know if you follow a gluten-free diet.

Millet: Another ancient grain that is really a seed, this one has a very light, mild flavor.

Oats (Old-Fashioned): Oats are wonderful for a million reasons. They are full of protein and fiber and contain beta-glucans, which can help regulate blood sugar. Great for breakfast, baking, and sweet applications, they work well as a filler and binder in savory foods!

Quinoa: This seed is gluten free, protein packed, and full of other important nutrients.

TVP (Texted Vegetable Protein): Derived from fat-free soy flour, TVP is a good source of fiber, complete protein, iron, magnesium, and phosphorous. It's also gluten free! I use this in the Peanut Butter Granola on page 43 for extra protein.

Wheat Germ: The heart of the wheat kernel where many minerals, vitamins, fatty acids, and fiber can be found is very toasty and delicious and adds a nutty depth to baked goods. It can be sprinkled on yogurt, or even used in place of breadcrumbs.

Whole-Wheat Flour: This ground wheat has all the nutritious bran and germ still intact.

Nuts and Seeds

Maybe I was a bird in a past life, because I really can't get enough nuts and seeds. Remember to STORE THEM IN YOUR FREEZER! This is a tip I learned from Martha—all nuts and seeds can go rancid very quickly in the pantry. Some of my favorite types are listed below:

Seeds: chia, flax, hemp, pepitas (pumpkin), poppy, sesame

Nuts: almonds, cashews, hazelnuts, pistachios (from Santa Barbara Pistachio Company), peanuts, walnuts (from K&K farms or Sierra Orchards), and Mediterranean pine nuts

Nuts should always be toasted. Set your oven to 425°F (220°C) and toast until golden and fragrant, 6 to 10 minutes. Make sure you set a timer. No one ever remembers to check on their nuts until they are already burning; it's just a fact.

Refrigerated Stuff

Citrus: Lemons, limes, and oranges are always great to have on hand for a squeeze over veggies, or to brighten up sauces and vinaigrettes with a bit of juice or zest.

Vegan/Non-Dairy Yogurt: I think I have tried every single vegan yogurt out there, and CocoJune coconut milk yogurt is the best-tasting option. KiteHill Greek Style Almond Milk Yogurt is a good alternative, if you're looking for something with a bit more protein.

Herbs: They are a fast path to fresh flavor and a way to dress up any dish.

Miso: All of the recipes in this book that call for miso use the mild white variety for that special umami funk.

Parmesan Cheese: Always keep a big chunk of good-quality aged Parm in your fridge.

Plain Unsweetened Greek-Style Yogurt: I keep yogurt in my fridge and use it in place of mayonnaise or sour cream, and in smoothies and sauces.

Tofu: Always try to buy organic, and if you see a locally made brand in stores, even better.

Tools

Cast-Iron Skillet: If you have only one pan, it should be this workhorse. It doesn't need to be fancy, just a 10- or 12-inch (25 to 20.5 cm) simple cast-iron pan.

Compost Bin: Keep a little bin on your counter and create your own compost situation or figure out what your local compost story is. Eating vegetable-forward foods creates a lot of future dirt!

Cutting Boards: I like to use one large wooden board and keep a smaller plastic board around for messy things like beets, flavorful ingredients like garlic and onions, or meat and fish.

Dutch Oven: I love using these heavy-bottomed pots with lids for making soups and stews.

Fine-Mesh Strainer: You'll be draining a lot of beans soon!

Fish Spatula: This flexible metal spatula is for so much more than fish.

Food Processor: This is great for making nut butters at home, and making quick work of grating vegetables and pureeing just about anything.

High-Powered Blender: If you're into health food, I think this is your first big kitchen purchase. A Vitamix blender is a big investment, but then you can always make your own nut milks, juices, smoothies—all for the price of about twenty-five smoothies from Erewhon!

Knives: If you get three knives, get a santoku, which is great for prepping vegetables; a paring knife for other little prep tasks; and a serrated bread knife for chopping nuts and slicing bread and baked goods.

OXO Julienne Peeler: Just order one right now! It takes up very little drawer space and will completely change your life (no matter how amazing your knife skills are).

Mandoline: Everyone is afraid of the mandoline, and it's understandable. My right thumb is a little misshapen. I get it. Just be careful. It's a really, really great tool that can save you so much time and make everything look a bit more elegant.

Microplane grater: I can't live without a Microplane. Citrus zest! Piles of Parmesan! Dashes of freshly ground nutmeg! Ginger!

Nut Milk Bag: It's not just for nut milk. Don't have a juicer? This is a great way to strain fresh vegetable juices that are made in the blender, so they are smooth and delicious.

OXO GreenSaver Produce Keeper: I love this breathable storage container. It seriously extends the shelf life of produce and has saved so many bundles of herbs and heads of lettuce from ending up as compost.

OXO Salad Spinner: Another desert island cooking tool for me, this makes quick work of washing and drying lettuce, greens, and herbs.

Parchment Paper Sheets: I buy unbleached parchment paper that is cut to the size of half-sheet pans from Amazon. I don't think it's laziness; I think it's smart. You'll never have to be frustrated with an unruly roll again. In Martha's test kitchen, we never let food come in direct contact with aluminum, so I habitually line baking sheets and foil with parchment.

Reusable Produce Bags: You'll get looks at the local co-op if you don't have these. But why not? It's such an easy way to use less unnecessary plastic.

Rice Cooker: If you're making a lot of rice, this takes a lot of guesswork out of it. And most models sing to you, which never is not entertaining.

Rimmed Baking Sheets: I don't think you can ever have enough. They are easy to store and transport, and great for baking and roasting—just about everything.

Spice Grinder or Mortar and Pestle: Either will do! When you are able to grind your own spices, you'll be amazed at how much more flavor they will have!

Spider: This is a must-have for deep-frying, wok-cooking, and soup-making.

Stockpot: Making your own stocks is so easy and makes a huge impact on the flavor of foods you're making. Get yourself a big ol' pot!

Tofu Press: If you have room in one of your cabinets and eat a lot of tofu, a tofu press is a great way to save on time and paper towels. Squeezing excess liquid out of tofu is a must for better texture and the ability to soak up even more flavor.

Tongs: Because you can't use your fingers for everything.

Y-Peeler: Once you've used a Y-peeler you won't even remember how to use a regular potato peeler or why you had one in the first place.

Food Vibrations

Go ahead, roll your eyes, turn the page, but I want to remind you that you should pay attention to the energy associated with the source, preparation, and eating of food.

Think about where your food comes from. Growing food is the best way to really feel a connection to where your ingredients originate—but going to a farmers' market and talking to someone else that did is pretty good too. I spend months growing my little tomato seedlings inside, then moving them out to the sun, waiting patiently for them to grow. The tomatoes are like my little children by the time they are ripe, and they could not be any more delicious, but it takes an incredible amount of effort and care for a single slice to be so good. Checking the label to see if a seedling is organic or googling whether it's in season locally or if it traveled halfway around the world to end up in your hands—that's taking care too. Go to the market yourself or take a second to appreciate whoever went there for you and filled your fridge. There is so much energy behind all of it.

Whatever energy goes into the food is what comes out of it. We used to call this "hate cooking" in the test kitchen. When the last thing you feel like doing is cooking and you are angry the whole time you're doing it, that's when things start to go wrong, things burn, you forget something, and then you end up even more frustrated. I've been there. I was there a few times developing this book. Trying to force it. But my kitchen mantra for a long time has been, "It's only food." And

it's important to remind yourself of that! I know it can feel like a lot of pressure to feed people, and like it's an emergency when something goes wrong—but people are always happy to be fed. It's really the thought that matters. Feeding someone is a gesture of love. Presenting it is a gesture of love as well. Adding a little fresh herb or lemon wedges and arranging it on the plate makes it more exciting to eat and makes people feel special. And to me, that's what it's all about. It can help if you think of the little prepping tasks in the kitchen as meditative, as a moment focused on yourself and your health, instead of a chore that is such a drag to deal with.

Take a breath (or even ten) before eating. As a cook, a large percentage of my meals are eating bites over the sink, or over the stove, or before something goes in the compost bin. Sometimes I eat a protein bar while I'm driving down the freeway before a shoot, and I almost always spill my coffee in the car. Sometimes I order in and watch *Frasier*, and sometimes I work while I eat and don't talk or make eye contact with my partner. But sometimes, my favorite times, are when I'm sitting with someone or a whole bunch of people at a table, with cloth napkins and the dishes I like—when we take a second to do a little cheers before we eat, make a little eye contact. Sometimes we take a couple of breaths. But it tastes better when you really get to slow down and savor every bite. The food satiates you much more quickly, without making you feel uncomfortably full. I think it's about pausing, before, during, and after the meal that helps me feel present.

IT IS EASY TO WRITE
A LOVE LETTER TO
CALIFORNIA

It is so easy to imagine the way it was in the 1930s, with its green hills and yellow mustard flowers and the fluorescent poppies and the narrow 110 with its arched tunnels and kinked exits. The craftsman bungalows lined up, lawns littered with oranges and lemons and grapefruits and loquats, rotting in the heat. California. You can taste the fruit, the sweet dates, the grassy juices, the quench. The sun hits differently; it almost pours onto you, and most days you don't feel guilty for relishing in it.

LA — it's easy to make fun of, but it's easy to love. There are vampires everywhere, and a lot of it is sitting back and watching, backing further into dark corners to observe exaggerated features, and the black devilish swizzle sticks swirling in drinks at Chateau Marmont — but there are also lucid-dreaming ceremonies in libraries painted thick with images of the occult from floor to ceiling, and the beach houses right along the PCH that are about to be swallowed up any day. Dolphins jumping in the waves at sunset while you watch with your toes in the sand, and David Hockney swimming pools. Sunglasses and convertibles and peeling off wetsuits. Palm trees that reached the sky decades ago lining the streets in Beverly Hills. Billboard after billboard after billboard after billboard on Sunset and David Lynch's weather report on KCRW. The fiery sun setting reflects on the large glass rectangular windows. Stars and crystals and the Hollywood sign and an almost constant cloud of marijuana smoke coming from . . . somewhere.

Sure, there is a hum of loneliness on some days. Slowness, almost swimming backwards. The staring-out-the-window kind of days when the weather hasn't changed in weeks, when you've forgotten what season it is and wonder what it's all about. But the lushness, the freshness, is persistent. The overwhelming scent of jasmine blooming, the agave busting from the sidewalk, the view of snowcapped mountains in the distance opposite the city. The sprouts and almonds and avocados, so many different kinds of avocados. Coming home and driving under the lemon tree and walking under cacti to the long table in the garden. Seeing that table full of people outside in the clean evening air. Speeding up the crazy driveway that is, every time, like a roller-coaster ride, because our house, like all these little houses, is teetering on the edge of the very top of a hill. Coming home to you, where the coyotes howl just outside.

BREAKFAST, SMOOTHIES & TONICS

I wouldn't mind if life were a perpetual Sunday morning. I'm slow to wake up every day, but on Sunday it doesn't matter. Maybe it's because we have blackout shades, or because I drift off every night to David Sedaris audiobooks and sleep so deeply that I rarely remember my dreams—but I'm lazy. I love those first fifteen, twenty, thirty minutes when the bed is still warm and the dogs are still floppy with their little chins resting on us, when I don't have to be up and moving. Long, messy breakfasts that stretch into the afternoons. I don't care much for lunch, or brunch. I'd take breakfast, sweet or savory, any day.

Someday I'll get into a routine where I hop out of bed into a cold-plunge pool and get back into meditating for twenty minutes before looking at my phone, but for now, one perfect latte and a healthy breakfast are things I try to do for myself every day.

When there isn't time for batters, and it's not an occasion calling for beet-cured salmon, there is granola and fruit, and there are smoothies. There are things that can be made ahead and eaten all week. Breakfast is a simple meal that my partner, Ben, who doesn't do much of the cooking, can make too, which I always appreciate.

Sometimes living in LA it feels like you can only get about one thing done per day. But I'm not going to talk anymore about slowing down, at the risk of entering Jack Johnson's "Banana Pancakes" territory, a song that sends a wave of panic through my body when I hear the opening strums. Instead, I'll hang on to my minor chords and existential dread and stand by the belief that what you put in your body first thing has a big impact on the way you feel in your brain and your body for the rest of the day.

●

Orange-Scented Tahini French Toast

Serves 4

My friend Ionut came back from Greece and couldn't stop eating toast drizzled with tahini and honey. This is the . . . decadent . . . version of his breakfast. Is this health food? I don't know. Is it healthier than thick slices of brioche dipped in butter and cream coated in powdered sugar and jam? I think so. This is a special breakfast and it's really worth making the homemade challah on page 262 to use for this French toast. Make two loaves and keep one in the freezer, so you have it on hand for next time.

....

PRODUCE
1 orange

PROTEIN
3 large eggs

PANTRY
½ cup (120 ml) canned coconut cream
Big pinch ground cinnamon
Pinch kosher salt
4 slices (1 inch/2.5 cm thick) Whole-Wheat
   Sesame Challah (page 262) or other tender
   bread (day-old is best)
¼ cup (40 g) sesame seeds
2 tablespoons olive oil or unsalted butter
¼ cup (60 ml) well-stirred tahini
4 teaspoons honey
Flaky sea salt, for finishing
Oranges, berries, or other fresh fruit (optional),
   for serving

Prep: In a large shallow bowl or baking dish, whisk together ½ cup (120 ml) coconut cream, 3 large eggs, zest of 1 orange, 1 big pinch cinnamon, and 1 pinch salt.

Working in batches, add 2 slices challah to the egg mixture. Let soak for about 15 minutes, then flip the slices and let soak for about 15 minutes more. (This may not take as long with day-or-two-old bread.) Meanwhile, heat a large cast-iron or nonstick skillet over medium and add the 2 tablespoons olive oil or butter.

Cook: Remove the bread from the egg mixture, allowing the excess to drip off, and place it in the pan. Meanwhile, add the remaining bread slices to the egg mixture to soak.

While the toast in the pan is cooking, sprinkle about 1 tablespoon of the sesame seeds over each piece to coat the side facing up. Take a little peek under the toast, and when the side facing down is a golden brown, about 2 minutes, carefully flip the toast and cook for about 2 to 3 minutes more. Repeat with the remaining 2 slices, adding a bit more oil or butter to the pan, if necessary.

Assemble and serve: Drizzle the toasts with a generous amount of tahini and honey, followed by a good sprinkle of flaky salt. Serve with oranges, berries, or other fresh fruit if desired.

Granolas

Crunchy Peanut Butter Granola

Makes 6 cups (730 g)

Every time I make this, Ben wishes there was somehow more peanut butter in it. I have maxed it out at an entire jar. This one is for peanut butter lovers everywhere. If you are a peanut allergic person, swap it out for almond, cashew, or sunflower butter. I like to leave as many big chunky pieces of granola as I can so that I can eat it right out of the bag, so mix gently without breaking it up too much. I also love it with milk and fresh strawberries or raspberries.

PROTEIN
4 large egg whites

PANTRY
1 (14-ounce/400 g) jar crunchy natural peanut butter
½ cup (120 ml) honey or brown rice syrup
1½ teaspoons kosher salt
1 cup (15 g) puffed millet
1 cup (15 g) puffed brown rice
1 cup (70 g) textured vegetable protein (TVP)
2 cups (180 g) old-fashioned (not thick-cut) oats

Prep: Preheat the oven to 325°F (165°C). Place a piece of parchment paper on a rimmed baking sheet.

Add 4 egg whites to a large bowl, followed by one 14-ounce (400 g) jar of peanut butter, ½ cup (75 ml) honey, and 1½ teaspoons salt. Whisk to combine. Add 1 cup (15 g) puffed millet, 1 cup (15 g) puffed brown rice, 1 cup (70 g) TVP, and 2 cups (180 g) oats and stir

together until well combined. Transfer to a baking sheet and spread into a thin, even layer.

Bake the granola: Bake for 15 minutes and then give the granola a good stir. Bake for another 15 minutes and stir again. It may be ready at this point, or it may need another 5 to 10 minutes. You're looking for golden brown and toasty. Let cool completely, then store in an airtight container for 3 to 4 weeks.

Dark Chocolate, Olive Oil, and Sea Salt Snacking Granola

Makes 6 cups (730 g)

This granola is really a snacking granola, the kind you eat by the handful while walking around the kitchen. It feels very rich and decadent, but not quite dessert material. I love Hu date-sweetened chocolate chips here, or Guittard's coconut-sugar chips.

PANTRY
½ cup (70 g) raw hazelnuts
2 cups (180 g) old-fashioned (not thick-cut) oats
¼ cup (30 g) unsweetened shredded coconut
½ cup (50 g) raw sliced almonds
¼ cup (40 g) sesame seeds
½ cup (45 g) unsweetened (100% cacao) dark chocolate chips or date-sweetened or coconut sugar–sweetened chocolate chips
¼ cup (30 g) cocoa nibs

(Continued)

From top: Crunchy Peanut Butter Granola, Golden Granola, and Dark Chocolate, Olive Oil, and Sea Salt Snacking Granola

¼ cup (25 g) cocoa powder
2 teaspoons vanilla extract
¼ cup (60 ml) olive oil
¼ cup (60 ml) maple syrup
1 teaspoon kosher salt

Prep: Preheat the oven to 325°F (165°C). Roughly chop ½ cup (70 g) hazelnuts. Line a rimmed baking sheet with parchment paper. In a large bowl, combine 2 cups (180 g) oats, ¼ cup (30 g) coconut, ½ cup (50 g) sliced almonds, ¼ cup (40 g) sesame seeds), ½ cup (45 g) chocolate chips, ¼ cup (30 g) cocoa nibs, ¼ cup (25 g) cocoa powder, 2 teaspoons vanilla, ¼ cup (60 ml) oil, ¼ cup (60 ml) maple syrup, and 1 teaspoon salt. Mix well. Transfer to a baking sheet.

Bake the granola: Bake for 15 minutes and then give the granola a good stir. Bake for another 15 minutes and stir again; the granola should be getting dry and toasty around the edges. At this point it may need another 5 to 10 minutes. The cocoa will look very dark, so taste it—the oats and nuts should be nice and toasty, but nothing should be burnt. Let cool completely, then store in an airtight container for 3 to 4 weeks.

Golden Granola

Makes 6 cups (730 g)

If I'm going to drink a latte, it needs to have caffeine, so the golden milk trend, where you combine turmeric, spices, and hot milk, has always eluded me. But I enjoy the flavors, and they are especially warming in the morning. This, I think, is a very nice way to experience them, especially with a big bowl of coconut yogurt and bright citrus.

DAIRY
4 large egg whites

PANTRY
1 cup (120 g) raw cashews
2 cups (180 g) old-fashioned (not thick-cut) oats

¼ cup (40 g) sesame seeds
¼ cup (40 g) golden flax seeds
¼ cup (40 g) chia seeds
1 teaspoon ground cinnamon
2 teaspoons ground ginger
1 tablespoon ground turmeric
⅓ cup (75 ml) coconut oil
¼ cup (60 ml) date syrup
1 teaspoon kosher salt
½ cup (45 g) coconut flakes
1 cup (150 g) dried golden berries
4 pitted, dried Medjool dates

Prep: Preheat the oven to 325°F (165°C). Line a rimmed baking sheet with parchment paper.

Roughly chop 1 cup (120 g) cashews. In a large bowl, combine 4 large egg whites, 2 cups (180 g) oats, ¼ cup (40 g) sesame seeds, ¼ cup (40 g) flax seeds, ¼ cup (40 g) chia seeds, 1 teaspoon cinnamon, 2 teaspoons ground ginger, 1 tablespoon turmeric, ⅓ cup (75 ml) coconut oil, ¼ cup (60 ml) date syrup, and 1 teaspoon kosher salt. Mix until combined and transfer to the prepared baking sheet.

Bake the granola: Bake for 15 minutes and then give the granola a good stir. Bake for another 15 minutes and stir again; it should be beginning to brown. Add ½ cup (45 g) coconut flakes and bake 10 to 15 minutes more, until the coconut is golden and toasty. Remove from the oven and stir in 1 cup (150 g) golden berries. Chop 4 Medjool dates and mix in. Let the granola cool completely. Transfer to an airtight container and store for up to 3 weeks.

Chai-Spiced Overnight Oats with Chia, Apple, Blackberries, and Figs

Serves 1

Overnight oats are one of the only things I can get myself together to prep the night before. It truly takes five minutes, and then breakfast is ready in the morning. You can throw in almost any fruit you have on hand and it will be delicious, but this is one of my favorite combinations. Almonds, raspberries, and cocoa nibs are some of my other favorite things to swirl in, as well as any nut butters I have on hand. Sometimes I make a few batches of this recipe, so I have breakfast ready for a few days (or a few people).

PRODUCE
1 apple
4 fresh or dried figs, halved (also delicious with plums)
Handful blackberries

PANTRY
½ cup (45 g) old-fashioned oats
3 teaspoons chia seeds
1 tablespoon date syrup, maple syrup, or honey, plus more if desired for the fruit
½ cup (120 ml) nut milk, store-bought or homemade (page 266)
Pinch ground cardamom
½ teaspoon ground cinnamon
¼ teaspoon ground ginger
Pinch kosher salt

Prep: Dice 1 apple. Halve 4 figs, or cut any other fruit you're using. In a small jar with a tight-fitting lid, add the apple, ¼ cup (20 g) of the oats, and sprinkle in 1½ teaspoons of the chia seeds.

Add half of the figs and a few of the blackberries to the oat mixture and give it a little mash. You can drizzle in a little date syrup too, to create kind of a compote situation, but it's optional. Top with the remaining ¼ cup (20 g) oats, 1½ teaspoons chia seeds, and fruit.

In a separate bowl, stir together ½ cup (120 ml) nut milk, 1 tablespoon date syrup, a pinch of ground cardamom, ½ teaspoon cinnamon, and ¼ teaspoon ginger, and a pinch of salt before pouring the mixture into the jar of oats. Cover the jar and refrigerate.

Chill and serve: Let the jar sit in the refrigerator for at least 2 hours before serving, but overnight is best. If you want to do a big batch, it will last in the fridge for about 3 days.

Fluffy Buckwheat Pancakes

Makes 12 (4-inch) pancakes

Growing up, I was completely unaware that fluffy buttermilk pancakes existed. I thought they were all thin, rubbery, dark gray, and made of buckwheat. I still prefer them dark gray and super nutty and toasty, but I've learned they can be light, thick, and fluffy too. I like to pile them up with cinnamon butter and a little drizzle of warm maple syrup. This version is vegan (and naturally gluten-free!), but feel free to swap the vegan ingredients for dairy if you prefer. Serve them with some fresh blueberries, or even some of the rhubarb ginger jam on page 252 for a sweet treat.

......

PRODUCE
¼ cup (60 ml) fresh lemon juice (from 1 lemon)
Fresh fruit, for serving, if desired

DAIRY
¾ cup (1½ sticks/170 g) vegan butter, ½ cup (115 g) softened, ¼ cup (55 g) melted

PANTRY
¼ cup (60 ml) plus 2 tablespoons maple syrup, plus more for serving
2 teaspoons ground cinnamon
¼ teaspoon plus pinch kosher salt
1 cup (120 g) buckwheat flour
1 cup (90 g) oat flour
4 teaspoons baking powder
4 teaspoons ground cinnamon
1½ cups (360 ml) nut milk, store-bought or homemade (page 266)
2 teaspoons vanilla extract
Neutral refined oil, such as sunflower or avocado

Make the cinnamon butter: In a small bowl, mix together ½ cup (115 g) softened butter, 2 tablespoons maple syrup, 2 teaspoons cinnamon, and a pinch of salt until well combined.

Prep the batter: In a large bowl, combine 1 cup (120 g) buckwheat flour, 1 cup (90 g) oat flour, 4 teaspoons baking powder, 2 teaspoons cinnamon, and ¼ teaspoon salt. Stir in 1½ cups (360 ml) nut milk, ¼ cup (60 ml) lemon juice, ¼ cup (60 ml) maple syrup, ¼ cup (55 g) melted butter, and 2 teaspoons vanilla and mix until all the ingredients are incorporated.

Cook the pancakes: Heat a large nonstick or cast-iron skillet over medium-low heat. Add a little bit of oil to the pan, if desired—but I tend to use a cast-iron skillet without oil. Now, ladle about ¼ cup (60 ml) batter into the pan—and be patient! Try not to mess with the heat or touch the pancake until you start to see a few bubbles forming in the center of the batter, which will take 30 seconds to 1 minute, depending on the heat. Add another pancake or two to the pan if they fit, but don't crowd it! When lots of bubbles are visible in the center of the pancakes, after 2 to 3 minutes, carefully flip, and cook for 1 to 3 minutes (you can peek a little bit on this side), until cooked through.

Serve: Top with maple syrup, cinnamon butter, and fresh fruit, if using.

Tip: Patience is the key to pancakes, especially fragile pancakes like these. It's better to go low and slow. Don't flip them too early, don't blast the heat to rush, and it's easier to work with smaller pancakes.

Morning Glory Muffins

Makes 18 muffins

If there was early-morning grocery shopping to do before work at Martha Stewart, I would always get myself a morning glory muffin at Whole Foods (and one for my friend Khalil!). Most muffins and morning pastries are filled with sugar and keep you satisfied for about two minutes, but classic morning glory muffins are filled with whole grains, fruit, carrots, and nuts and are perfect for breakfast on the go. Also, it is delicious with cinnamon butter (see page 49).

....

PRODUCE
4 large carrots (about 8 ounces/200 g total)
1 apple, such as Honeycrisp
¼ cup (60 ml) fresh orange juice (from 1 orange)

PROTEIN
3 large eggs

PANTRY
2 cups (250 g) whole-wheat flour
¼ cup (30 g) wheat germ
1 tablespoon ground cinnamon
1 teaspoon baking soda
½ teaspoon kosher salt
½ cup (45 g) unsweetened shredded coconut
½ cup (70 g) raisins
½ cup (60 g) pecans, toasted (see page 33)
1 cup (190 g) pitted, dried Medjool dates
1 cup (240 ml) hot water
1 teaspoon vanilla extract
½ cup (120 ml) refined coconut oil or neutral oil, such as sunflower or avocado

Prep: Preheat the oven to 350°F (175°C). Prepare 18 muffin tins with liners.

In a large bowl, combine 2 cups (250 g) whole-wheat flour, ¼ cup (30 g) wheat germ, 1 tablespoon cinnamon, 1 teaspoon baking soda, ½ teaspoon kosher salt, ½ cup (45 g) unsweetened shredded coconut,

½ cup (70 g) raisins, and ½ cup (60 g) pecans. Whisk and set aside.

In the bowl of a food processor, combine 1 cup (190 g) pitted Medjool dates and 1 cup (240 ml) hot water. Let sit for at least 5 minutes before blending into a smooth paste, scraping down the sides as necessary. Transfer the date paste to another large bowl, and then attach the grater attachment to the food processor (you can also grate by hand if you prefer). Shred 4 carrots (you should end up with about 2¼ cups/200 g). Peel, core, and dice 1 apple, and add the carrots and apple to the bowl with the date paste.

Add 3 large eggs, 1 teaspoon vanilla, ½ cup (120 ml) coconut or neutral oil, and ¼ cup (60 ml) orange juice to the bowl with the date paste and stir to combine.

Fold the wet mixture into the dry mixture until combined. Use a 2-ounce (60 ml) ice cream scoop to portion out 18 heaping scoops, about ⅓ cup (80 ml) each, for perfect little muffins in the prepared tins.

Cook: Bake for 25 to 28 minutes, until a toothpick inserted in the center comes out clean. The cooled muffins can be sealed in an airtight container for up to a week, or frozen and enjoyed up to 3 months later.

Melon Salad with Honey, Pistachio Yogurt, and Mint

Serves 2 to 4

Melon is usually just a little side dish for breakfast, but in the summer months when it's bright and sunny and hot and sticky, ripe melons are so incredibly sweet and juicy, they are really all I want. Swirling deep green pistachio butter into rich yogurt sweetened with honey makes a simple fruit salad feel luxurious.

....

PRODUCE
1 ripe cantaloupe
Handful fresh mint leaves
1 lime

DAIRY
1 cup (240 ml) plain unsweetened Greek yogurt

PANTRY
2 tablespoons Nut Butter (preferably pistachio; page 266)
1 tablespoon honey
Extra-virgin olive oil
Flaky salt, for serving
Crushed pistachios, for serving

Prep: Cut both ends off the melon so it can stand up straight. Move the knife around the curve of the melon to cut off the white rind. Cut the melon in half, remove the seeds, and thinly slice.

Stir together 1 cup (240 ml) yogurt, 2 tablespoons nut butter, and 1 tablespoon honey.

Assemble and serve: Spread the yogurt mixture on the bottom of the plate and arrange the sliced melon over the top. Squeeze a bit of lime juice and finish with a drizzle of extra-virgin olive oil and sprinkle with flaky salt, crushed pistachios, and fresh mint leaves.

Savory Brown Rice Porridge with Greens and Soft Egg

Serves 6 to 8

Congee, a savory rice porridge, is a classic Chinese breakfast, a staple in many Asian countries, and truly one of the ultimate comfort foods. Warming, nourishing, and incredibly tasty, a big pot of congee can last for days. Serve with whatever toppings you like. For a vegetarian version use vegetable or mushroom stock, and stir in sliced mushrooms instead of using chicken thighs.

PRODUCE
1 bunch green onions
2-inch (5 cm) piece fresh ginger
2 handfuls of greens, such as spinach, mustard, or Swiss chard

PROTEIN
6 to 8 large eggs
2 pounds (910 g) bone-in skinless chicken thighs

PANTRY
Neutral oil, such as sunflower or avocado
8 cups (2 liters) chicken stock, store-bought or homemade (page 265)
1 cup (185 g) short-grain brown rice
Kosher salt
Toasted sesame oil, for serving
Chili crisp, for serving (page 169)

Cook: In a large heavy-bottomed enamel cast-iron or other large pot, add a little drizzle of neutral oil and heat over medium. Thinly slice just the white parts of the bunch of green onions and reserve the greens. Peel the 2-inch (5 cm) piece ginger and cut into matchsticks or finely chop. Add the white parts of the green onion and the ginger to the pot and cook until soft, about 3 minutes.

Add 8 cups (2 liters) chicken stock, 1 cup (185 g) brown rice, and 2 pounds (910 g) bone-in skinless chicken

thighs to the pot and bring the stock to a boil. Reduce the heat to a simmer, cover, and cook for 45 minutes, checking on the mixture occasionally to make sure it's not boiling.

Carefully remove the chicken from the pot and set on a plate to cool. Once it is cool, shred the chicken and store it, covered, in the fridge while you continue cooking the rice.

Continue simmering the porridge, uncovered, and stirring occasionally until it is looking super creamy, which could take 1½ to 2 hours.

Return the chicken to the pot, cook until warmed through, and season with salt to taste.

Prepare an ice bath by filling a large bowl with ice water. Bring a medium pot of water to a boil. Gently lower 6 to 8 large eggs into the pot and cook for 7 minutes, until soft-boiled. Transfer to the ice bath, and then peel the eggs when cool enough to handle.

Assemble and serve: Slice the green portion of the green onions. Serve the rice porridge with the soft-boiled eggs, green onion, and toasted sesame oil and chili crisp to taste. Store in an airtight container for up to 5 days. Reheat on the stovetop or in the microwave, adding a bit of water if necessary to thin to desired consistency.

Beet-Cured Salmon and Jammy Egg Toasts

Serves 6 to 12

The truth is I think that it takes less time to prep this salmon (which will truly blow away all of your brunch guests) than it does to stand in line for freshly sliced lox at Russ & Daughters. Grated beets not only add a delicious, sweet flavor to the salmon, but they also turn it the most brilliant pink color, making it fit for a holiday meal (or just any weekend get together).

PRODUCE
4 lemons
4 large beets
2 cups (60 g) chopped fresh dill, plus sprigs for
  serving

DAIRY
1 cup Fennel Tzatziki (page 143) or your favorite
  cream cheese

PROTEIN
2 pounds (910 g) wild salmon fillet, skin removed
1 dozen large eggs

PANTRY
1 cup (200 g) kosher salt
1 cup (200 g) organic cane sugar
8 slices Nordic seed bread
Capers, flaky salt, everything seasoning, and
  freshly ground black pepper, for serving

Prep the salmon: Pat 2 pounds (910 g) skinless salmon fillet dry with paper towels. In a small bowl, combine 1 cup (200 g) salt, 1 cup (200 g) sugar, and the zest of 4 lemons.

Peel and shred 4 large beets (about 8 ounces/250 g) on the large holes of the box grater. Spread half of the salt mixture over the top and edges of the salmon and pat it so it really sticks. Sprinkle half of the chopped dill over

the salmon and coat with half of the shredded beets, pressing again to make sure the dill and beets stick to the salmon.

Carefully flip the salmon and set it on a large piece of plastic wrap with the coating side down. Coat the other side of the salmon with the other half of the salt mixture, chopped dill, and beets, as described above. Wrap the salmon tightly in the plastic, set on a large plate or a quarter sheet tray, and let sit in the fridge for at least 24 hours but preferably 48 hours. (Don't skip the sheet pan! The beet juice has a tendency to creep out of the plastic wrap, and you don't want a big spill in your fridge!!!)

Cook the eggs: When ready to serve, fill a large bowl with ice water. Bring a medium pot of water to a boil. Gently lower 12 large eggs into the pot and cook for 7 minutes, until soft-boiled. Transfer to the ice bath, and then peel the eggs when cool enough to handle.

Assemble and serve: When you are ready to serve the salmon, wipe off the outside coating completely and thinly slice it, about ¼ inch (5 mm) thick.

Arrange the toasted seed bread on a work surface or tray. Spread about 1 tablespoon fennel tzatziki on each slice of toast, then top with a few slices cured salmon. Finish each one with capers, fresh dill, and a soft egg. Sprinkle with flaky salt, season with everything seasoning and freshly ground black pepper, and serve.

Asparagus, Pea, and Crispy Leek Frittata

Serves 8

Frittatas are the easiest and best for a brunch when people are coming over. I'm always tempted to drizzle a little something spicy over this one, like chili crisp, or put it on a freshly baked roll with a bit of aioli, but plain, it really tastes like spring. And it's pretty wonderful not messing with that.

....

PRODUCE
1 recipe Crispy Leeks (page 265; reserve the leek-
    infused cooking oil)
½ bunch asparagus
½ cup (75 g) English peas (frozen is fine)
2 handfuls baby arugula

DAIRY
2 ounces (55 g) soft young sheep's milk cheese or
    Bulgarian feta

PROTEIN
12 large eggs

PANTRY
Extra-virgin olive oil
Kosher salt and freshly ground black pepper
Chili crisp, store-bought or homemade (page 169)
    (optional)

Prep: Make the crispy leeks (see page 265).

Preheat the oven to 425°F (220°C). Keep a little bit (about 2 tablespoons) of the leek-infused oil in the cast-iron skillet.

Shave the asparagus stalks as much as you can into thin ribbons using a Y-peeler. Cut any middle bits into 1-inch (2.5 cm) pieces. Trim off the tips. Add the tips and bits to the pan and sauté briefly, about 1 minute, just until they are bright green. Add the ribbons and turn off the heat.

Whisk the eggs really well in a large bowl and season with salt and pepper. Add ½ cup (75 g) peas and one handful arugula and pour the eggs into the skillet. Bring the heat back up to medium. Cook, moving everything around with a rubber spatula until the edges of the frittata are set, 5 to 7 minutes.

Bake: Add 2 ounces (55 g) cheese to the top of the frittata in little chunks. Sprinkle with the crispy leeks, cover with a piece of foil, and carefully transfer to the preheated oven. Bake until just set, 8 to 10 minutes. Top with the remaining handful of arugula, then slice and serve with chili crisp, if desired.

BEN HAS A 1990 VW WESTFALIA

that maxes out at 55 on the highway. The thing about the van is it forces you to slow down (exactly what I need). The big windshield makes you look out at the mountains, the ocean, the little yellow mustard flowers on the side of the road. There is no AC, so you have to roll the windows down and feel the wind and hear the sound of other cars blowing past you. It only has a CD player, so you HAVE to listen to Sublime's *40oz. to Freedom* and Green Day's *Dookie*.

The van has a little kitchen with a two-burner stove and a big sliding door that you can open up to get a perfect view of the landscape wherever you decide to park and cook. The front seats spin around, so you can sit at a little table for two. When Ben sliced up fresh scallops at the beach (yes there is a little fridge onboard) with a big squeeze of lime juice, I think right then and there it convinced me to stay in LA forever.

Breakfast is our favorite meal to make on the road — simple, filling things like the shakshuka on the next page. We always pack granola (page 43), the Overnight Oats (page 46) are great too, or a batch of Morning Glory Muffins (page 50), which can even be griddled with a little bit of butter. I guess it's pretty cozy for camping.

Spicy Harissa and Cherry Tomato Shakshuka

Serves 2 to 4

This is the breakfast I like to make when we're on the road. It's an easy one for when you're traveling, because mostly everything is a pantry ingredient, and it all gets made in a single pan. It's good for a group. It's super satisfying, and it keeps you full for a long time. It has a lot of lusciousness going on with the olive oil, yogurt, and soft egg yolks, and feels decadent and fancy when it's really simple to pull together. Sometimes I add a little cumin or coriander seeds or a pinch of cinnamon or saffron, but it's not necessary. I love the canned cherry tomatoes for their sweet flavor and their texture; they break down just enough.

....

PRODUCE
½ medium yellow onion
2 cloves garlic
Fresh herbs, such as parsley, dill, and cilantro, for
   serving

DAIRY
Sheep's milk yogurt or feta cheese, for serving

PROTEIN
4 to 6 large eggs

PANTRY
Extra-virgin olive oil
Kosher salt and freshly ground black pepper
2 to 3 tablespoons harissa paste (depending on
   how spicy you want it!)
1 (14-ounce/400 g) can cherry tomatoes

Prep: Thinly slice ½ onion and 2 cloves garlic.

Cook: In a cast-iron or other straight-sided skillet, add a good drizzle of olive oil and heat over medium-high. Add the onions and garlic. Cook, stirring, until the onions are soft and translucent. Don't rush this part! Really let them cook; this can take about 8 minutes. Season with salt.

Add 2 to 3 tablespoons harissa and stir around a bit. Let cook for a minute or two before adding the can of tomatoes with their juices.

Break up the tomatoes a bit with a wooden spoon, and then simmer the mixture until the tomatoes have reduced into a thick, flavorful sauce. Using a wooden spoon, working with one egg at a time, create individual wells for 4 to 6 large eggs and crack an egg into each well. Sprinkle each egg with a little salt and pepper. Cover the shakshuka and let simmer until the egg whites are completely opaque, but the yolks are still soft, 7 to 10 minutes.

Garnish and serve: Serve topped with dollops of Greek yogurt and fresh herbs and eat it somewhere along the Pacific Coast Highway if you can.

Masala-Spiced Potato Hash with Spinach and Yogurt

Serves 4

I worked in a surf shop in high school in Amagansett Square, two doors down from Hampton Chutney Co., which made an incredible breakfast dosa that I would get most mornings. When I'm cooking for myself, I'm a little too lazy and impatient to think ahead to make dosa batter, even though it's absolutely worth doing, so here are my favorite flavors of that dosa, simplified. I also got mine with avocado and Jack cheese back then, which is in no way authentic, but in every way delicious.

....

PRODUCE
3 large Yukon gold potatoes (about 1½ pounds/ 680 g total)
2-inch (5 cm) piece fresh ginger
1 shallot
1 serrano chile
2 big handfuls baby spinach
Fresh cilantro leaves, for serving

DAIRY
Unsweetened plain or coconut yogurt, for serving

PROTEIN
4 large eggs

PANTRY
Kosher salt
2 tablespoons ghee or coconut oil, plus more if needed
½ teaspoon brown mustard seeds
½ teaspoon cumin seeds
½ teaspoon ground turmeric

Prep: Peel 3 potatoes, cut them into 2-inch (5 cm) chunks, and add them to a pot. Cover with water by 2 inches (5 cm), add a good pinch of salt, and bring to a boil over medium-high heat. Boil until tender when pierced with a knife, about 5 to 7 minutes. Reserve about 1 cup of the cooking liquid and drain.

Peel and mince the 2 inches (5 cm) fresh ginger. Thinly slice a shallot and a serrano chile.

Cook: In a large cast-iron skillet, heat 2 tablespoons ghee or oil over medium heat, add the ginger, shallot, and half of the sliced serrano chile and cook just until softened, about 3 minutes. Add ½ teaspoon mustard seeds and ½ teaspoon cumin seeds and cook just until they begin to sizzle, about 20 seconds.

Add the boiled potatoes, ½ teaspoon turmeric, a big pinch of salt, and a little additional ghee or oil if it seems dry. Mash the potatoes a bit with a fork or wooden spoon and cook for about 4 to 5 minutes, so they brown in spots. Add 2 handfuls baby spinach and a bit of the reserved potato cooking water.

Once the spinach is wilted, season to taste, make 4 little wells, and crack one egg into each well. Season the eggs with salt and pepper, cover, and cook. After about 2 minutes, check under the lid to make sure that the bottom of the hash isn't burning and adjust the heat if needed.

Assemble and serve: Assemble the bowls with steamed vegetables, eggs, and beans. When the egg whites are opaque but the yolks are still runny, after about 5 to 8 minutes total, remove the pan from the heat, add a few dollops of yogurt, and sprinkle with the remaining chile and some fresh cilantro leaves.

Black Bean, Sweet Potato, and Greens Breakfast Bowl

Serves 4

A breakfast burrito minus the tortilla, this is one of my favorite satisfying bowls that keeps me full all day. Sometimes I add brown rice to the bottom, and I always add a generous amount of hot sauce.

....

PRODUCE
½ red onion
2 limes
3 medium sweet potatoes
1 (1-pound/454 g) bunch collard greens, Swiss chard, or kale
Handful fresh cilantro
1 avocado
2 radishes

PANTRY
2 (14-ounce/400 g) cans black beans
Kosher salt and freshly ground black pepper
Extra-virgin olive oil
Benny's Green Salsa (page 146) or Salsa Macha (page 276)
Hot sauce of choice

PROTEIN
6 large eggs

DAIRY
¼ cup (60 ml) plain Greek-style yogurt

Pickle the onion: Thinly slice ½ red onion and place in a small bowl. Squeeze the juice of 1 lime over the onion and toss with a bit of salt.

Prep and steam the produce: Cut 3 sweet potatoes into a 1-inch (2.5 cm) dice. Remove any thick stems from one bunch of collard greens and chop the leaves into 1-inch (2.5 cm) pieces.

Fill a large pot with 2 inches (5 cm) water and place a steamer basket inside the pot. Add the sweet potatoes and bring to a boil. Reduce to a simmer, cover, and cook until the potatoes are tender, 7 to 8 minutes. Push them to one side, add the greens, and cook for 5 minutes, until tender.

Warm the beans: Drain and rinse two (14-ounce/ 400 g) cans of black beans. Add to a small pot with ¼ cup (60 ml) water, and bring to a simmer over medium heat. Continue to cook until warmed through and softened, about 15 minutes.

Scramble the eggs: Crack 6 large eggs into a medium bowl. Season well with salt and pepper and whisk until blended. Heat a medium skillet over medium heat and add a generous glug of olive oil. Add the eggs and cook, pushing them from the edges inward with a rubber spatula. Keep moving the scrambled eggs in the pan until they are completely set, about 4 minutes. Transfer immediately to the assembled breakfast bowls.

Assemble and serve: Thinly slice 1 avocado and 2 radishes. Top the bowls with avocado, pickled onion, radishes, salsa, yogurt, and cilantro. Serve with your favorite hot sauce and lime wedges.

Opposite: Creamsicle Smoothie
Clockwise from top: Maca, Mocha,
and Mushroom; PB and J; and
Sweet Potato Pie Smoothies

Smoothies

Creamsicle Smoothie

Serves 2

This smoothie falls somewhere in between a mango lassi and an Orange Julius; it's bright, a little tangy, just sweet enough, and super creamy. It's very sunshiney, and delicious any time of year, but is really a boost during the winter months when citrus is in season. I spoon a little fresh passion fruit on top when it's in season. For protein I like the natural, unsweetened, plant-based Orgain Organic Protein, or KOS Organic Plant Protein.

PRODUCE
2 seedless oranges
½ cup (85 g) frozen mango chunks
1 frozen banana
2-inch (5 cm) piece fresh turmeric root, 2 ounces (60 ml) turmeric juice, or 1 teaspoon ground turmeric

DAIRY
½ cup (120 ml) unsweetened plain or coconut yogurt
¼ cup (60 ml) nut milk, store-bought or homemade (page 266); or coconut cream

PANTRY
1 scoop vanilla protein powder, if desired
1 teaspoon vanilla extract
2 tablespoons canned coconut cream, for garnish

Prep and blend: Peel three strips of zest from one of the oranges with a Y-peeler and add to the blender. Carefully cut off the ends of each orange, and then, hugging the curves of the orange, cut off the pith and rind, revealing the flesh. Add the naked oranges to the blender. Add ½ cup (85 g) frozen mango chunks, 1 frozen banana, 2-inch (5 cm) piece fresh turmeric root, 1 scoop vanilla protein powder, 1 teaspoon vanilla, ½ cup (120 ml) plain or coconut yogurt, and ½ cup (120 ml) nut milk and blend until very smooth.

Pour and serve: Using a spoon, pour a little coconut cream into the middle of a glass and continue all the way around to coat the sides. Repeat with the second glass. Pour in the smoothies and brighten up your day (and someone else's) a little bit.

PB and J Smoothie

Serves 1 or 2

Apples add a healthy dose of fiber and bulk up this smoothie without adding a ton of extra calories or sugar. Switch the blueberries for raspberries or strawberries if that's what you have on hand. Also throw in a handful of baby spinach if you need to get some greens in; it won't be a beautiful color, but it will taste great.

PRODUCE
1 tart apple, such as Granny Smith or Honeycrisp
1 frozen banana
¼ cup (40 g) frozen wild blueberries

DAIRY
½ cup (120 ml) unsweetened plain or coconut yogurt

PANTRY
¼ cup (60 ml) nut milk, store-bought or homemade (page 266)
2 big spoonfuls creamy peanut butter

2 scoops vanilla protein powder
Pinch ground cinnamon

Prep: Chop a tart apple and add the pieces to a blender.

Blend: Add 1 frozen banana, ¼ cup (40 g) blueberries, ½ cup (120 ml) yogurt, ½ cup (120 ml) almond milk, 2 big spoonfuls peanut butter, 2 scoops protein powder, and one pinch cinnamon to the blender. Blend until smooth, adding a bit of water if necessary to reach desired consistency.

Pour and serve: Divide between two glasses or pour it into one and drink it all yourself.

Sweet Potato Pie Smoothie

Serves 1 or 2

I worked on an amazing kids' cooking show with the pastry chef Duff Goldman and the Henson Puppets. The puppets couldn't be around food, but every morning Duff would make a smoothie with raw sweet potato, and I was fascinated. Cutting sweet potatoes into cubes and blending them in a high-powered blender yields a mild-tasting, creamy smoothie that has a mild sweetness and the spice of a sweet potato pie that is NOT the texture of baby food.

PRODUCE
1 small sweet potato
1 frozen banana

DAIRY
¼ cup (60 ml) unsweetened plain or coconut yogurt
¼ cup (60 ml) nut milk, store-bought or homemade (page 266)

PANTRY
¼ teaspoon ground cinnamon
Pinch ground ginger

Prep: Finely dice 1 small sweet potato.

Blend: In a blender, combine the sweet potato, 1 frozen banana, ¼ cup (60 ml) yogurt, ½ cup (120 ml) almond milk, ¼ teaspoon cinnamon, and a pinch ginger. Blend until smooth.

Pour and serve: Pour into one glass or divide between two and enjoy.

Maca, Mocha, Mushroom Smoothie

Serves 1 or 2

This smoothie is jet fuel. Use on busy mornings, before a workout, or to help you reach any quickly approaching deadlines (like I did). Medicinal mushrooms are so incredible and beneficial I take a supplement every day. Make sure to look for a mushroom supplement with a verified active compound made from fruiting bodies and check that there is no starch, grains, or mycelium in the ingredient list. I love Real Mushrooms 5 Defenders powder or Mālama Mushrooms 8 Mushrooms Superfood Powder.

PRODUCE
1 frozen banana

PANTRY
1 shot espresso or 2 tablespoons (30 ml) strong brewed coffee or cold brew
½ teaspoon mushroom powder, such as Real Mushrooms or Mālama Mushrooms
2 teaspoons cocoa powder
1 teaspoon maca powder
¼ cup (60 ml) nut milk, store-bought or homemade (page 266)
2 pitted, dried Medjool dates
Handful ice, if desired

Blend and serve: Add all ingredients to a blender and blend until smooth. Pour into glass(es) and drink up.

Bones and Grass

Serves 2

In 2018 Ben moved into a new apartment in Bed-Stuy, a little treehouse on the top floor.
He was getting ready for a new season of his show *High Maintenance* where he had some scenes
on a paddleboard, and we would work out on the roof a lot and drink this every morning.
It was a real health kick. We were making our own nut milk every week. It didn't last long, but
it was a good routine, and I think back on that time fondly. No one would like the version we drank,
so I improved it, and now it's perfect, landing somewhere between a smoothie and a matcha latte,
and is something you'll want to make part of your daily routine.

....

PRODUCE
1 banana
1 tart apple, such as Granny Smith or Honeycrisp
1 handful baby spinach

PANTRY
1 cup (240 ml) nut milk, store-bought or
    homemade (page 266)
1 pitted, dried Medjool date
2 teaspoons ceremonial-grade matcha powder
8 tablespoons (40 g) collagen peptides
2 teaspoons maca powder

Prep: Peel and slice the banana. Cut the cheeks off the apple.

Blend: Combine all the ingredients in a blender, blend until smooth, and divide between two glasses.

Tonics

Beet Shrub

Makes 1½ cups (355 ml)

This started as a cocktail recipe, which didn't seem to belong in a health food book. But as a tonic with sparkling water, this is an absolutely delicious beverage. And if you did want to use this shrub in a cocktail, having beet juice in it doesn't hurt, right? To make the simple syrup, just heat 1 cup (240 ml) water over medium and stir in 1 cup (200 g) sugar until dissolved.

PRODUCE
1 beet
1 Honeycrisp apple
1 lemon

PANTRY
¼ cup (60 ml) apple cider vinegar or Rose Vinegar (page 269)
1 cup (240 ml) simple syrup
Sparkling water

Prep: Peel and chop 1 beet and 1 apple. Cut the peel and pith away from 1 lemon and remove any visible seeds.

Blend: Add the beet, apple, lemon, ¼ cup (60 ml) apple cider vinegar, and 1 cup (240 ml) simple syrup to a blender and blend until very smooth. Strain through a fine-mesh sieve and transfer to an airtight container. Refrigerate for at least one week, but two or three is even better.

Assemble and serve: When you are ready to enjoy the shrub, for each serving, pour about ¼ cup (60 ml) over ice and top with the sparkling water.

Test Kitchen Turmeric

Serves 6

In the test kitchen at Martha Stewart, whenever cold season came upon us, someone (usually Shira, Laura, or Geri), would make a big batch of this tonic daily. Just a couple of tablespoons mixed with sparkling water is like drinking a big glass of sunshine. Add a little ginger or orange juice as well if you have some on hand.

PRODUCE
4 ounces (115 g) fresh turmeric root
2 lemons

PANTRY
¼ cup (60 ml) honey
Ice, for serving
Sparkling water, for serving

Prep: Peel and chop 4 ounces (115 g) fresh turmeric. Juice 2 lemons.

Blend: Add the turmeric to a juicer or blender (be very careful, this juice can stain EVERYTHING). If using a juicer, simply juice the turmeric. If blending, puree until smooth, adding a little bit of water, if necessary, to achieve a nice juice consistency. Pour into a glass container and mix in the lemon juice and ¼ cup (60 ml) honey.

Assemble and serve: For a single serving, spoon about 1 ounce (30 ml) tonic over ice and top with sparkling water. Store the rest in an airtight container for up to 5 days.

Martha's Green Juice

Serves 2

Every single morning Martha Stewart starts her day with a glass of this green juice and a whole milk cappuccino. And of course, it's the perfectly balanced green juice—while it changes a little bit here and there, one constant is that it's always spinach and never kale (which tastes too earthy). This juice is just sweet enough, not bitter at all, and it seems pretty evident that adding it to your routine may give you eternal youth.

PRODUCE
1 Granny Smith apple
2 stalks celery
2-inch (5 cm) piece fresh ginger
1 orange
1 English cucumber
½ bunch fresh flat-leaf parsley
2 big handfuls baby spinach

Prep the fruits and vegetables: Cut the cheeks off 1 apple and add them to a juicer or blender. Cut 2 celery stalks in half and add to the blender or juicer. Peel a 2-inch (5 cm) piece fresh ginger and add. Peel off 3 strips zest from the orange and add to the juicer or blender, then carefully trim the remaining pith and peel from the orange and add the flesh to the juicer or blender. Cut 1 cucumber into pieces if necessary to fit into your juicer or blender.

Blend or juice: Add ½ bunch fresh parsley, and 2 big handfuls baby spinach to the juicer or blender.

If using a juicer, simply juice and serve immediately. If blending, puree until smooth, adding a little bit of water if necessary to achieve a nice juice consistency, then squeeze through a nut milk bag or fine-mesh strainer, and serve.

BEANS & LEGUMES

My friends are really into beans. Some are members of exclusive bean clubs with long wait lists to become a member; others have tried to form love connections over a mutual obsession with legumes. My friend Jason survives exclusively off rice and beans and wouldn't have it any other way. I could go on and on, really, but instead I'll let the beans do the talking.

Beans are cheap, delicious, and extremely nutritious and are a vital part of a plant-based diet, because they are amazing sources of protein, fiber, vitamins, and minerals. The dishes in this chapter are extremely satisfying and filling, and a great way to incorporate beans into your diet whether you're already a bean lover or you still need some convincing.

People's opinions about soaking beans are all over the place, but I like to do it, as soaked beans require less actual cooking time and are easier to digest. So, try to soak the beans in cold water for at least 8 hours or overnight. If you don't, be aware that the cooking time may be longer, but see page 271 for a guide to timing and other helpful information about using beans in the following recipes.

Cauliflower and Chickpea Curry

Serves 4

Everyone needs a good curry recipe up their sleeve—one that hits the spot every single time. I love this one because it's not too soupy, just rich enough, and has so many fiber-rich ingredients it keeps you satisfied for a really long time. I always bug my friend Anand when my Indian-inspired recipes need tweaking, and he always pulls through with his mom's secrets. In this case, a good amount of rich coconut milk and tomato paste does the trick.

PRODUCE
1 yellow onion
3 cloves garlic
1-inch (2.5 cm) piece fresh ginger
1 large head cauliflower
5 ounces (140 g) fresh baby spinach
Fresh cilantro, for serving

PANTRY
3 tablespoons ghee or coconut oil
1 teaspoon ground turmeric
1 teaspoon ground cumin
1 teaspoon ground coriander
½ teaspoon chile powder, such as Kashmiri, or a
    pinch of cayenne
Kosher salt
2 tablespoons tomato paste
1 (14-ounce/400 ml) can unsweetened coconut
    milk
1 (14-ounce/400 g) can chickpeas
Steamed white or brown basmati rice, for serving
Whole-wheat naan, for serving

Prep the produce: Chop 1 onion and 3 cloves garlic and peel and mince a 1-inch (2.5 cm) piece fresh ginger. Cut 1 large head of cauliflower into 1-inch (2.5 cm) florets.

Cook the curry: Heat a large deep skillet or a heavy-bottomed pot over medium-high and add 3 tablespoons ghee or coconut oil. Add the onion and cook until soft and translucent, about 7 minutes. Add the garlic and ginger and cook for another minute, just until fragrant. Add 1 teaspoon turmeric powder, 1 teaspoon ground cumin, 1 teaspoon ground coriander, ½ teaspoon chile powder, and a good amount of kosher salt. Cook until fragrant, about 2 minutes.

Add 2 tablespoons tomato paste and cook for a few minutes, until the color has deepened a little bit and it no longer has a raw taste, about 2 minutes. Add one 14-ounce (400 ml) can coconut milk, the cauliflower florets, and one 14-ounce (400 g) can chickpeas to the pot. Stir, and cook until the cauliflower is tender and the sauce is thick and slightly reduced, about 10 minutes.

Finish and serve: Stir in 5 ounces (140 g) spinach and cook until just wilted. Serve with brown basmati rice, whole-wheat naan, and some fresh cilantro.

Beet and Black Bean Burgers with Sweet Potato Fries

Serves 6 as a meal

I want a veggie burger that tastes like vegetables, really flavorful delicious vegetables full of texture. Beets, carrots, walnuts, and sunflower seeds add just a little tooth here, black beans and oats make it fiber rich and satisfying, and chipotle chiles add a smoky kick. Sweet potato fries are just roasted sweet potatoes cut into fry shapes, so they are healthy enough to be part of this book and make this an incredibly satisfying vegan meal.

....

PRODUCE
½ yellow onion
2 medium carrots (about 5¼ ounces/150 g total)
1 medium beet (about 7 ounces/200 g)
1 handful fresh cilantro leaves
2 medium sweet potatoes (about 30 ounces/ 850 g total)
1 red onion
Alfalfa or broccoli sprouts, for serving

PANTRY
2 tablespoons flaxseed meal or 1 large egg
1 (14-ounce/400 g) can black beans
1 cup (90 g) old-fashioned oats
½ cup (75 g) roasted sunflower seeds
½ cup (50 g) walnuts, toasted (see page 33)
1 tablespoon soy sauce or liquid aminos
2 large chipotle chiles in adobo, with seeds, or 1 heaping teaspoon chipotle chile powder
1½ teaspoons kosher salt
Extra-virgin olive oil
1 tablespoon cornstarch
Flaky salt
12 slices seeded bread, buns, or English muffins, for serving
Avocado Crema (page 273)

Prep the burgers: Make the flaxseed "egg" by mixing 2 tablespoons flaxseed meal with 5 tablespoons of warm water. Let sit while you prep.

Drain and rinse one 14-ounce (400 g) can black beans. Roughly chop ½ yellow onion. Using the grating attachment of a food processor, shred 2 medium carrots and then 1 medium beet. Transfer the veggies to a bowl while you use the regular blade to chop up some of the other ingredients.

Add the oats next and pulse until mostly ground up—a little texture is fine. Add the beans and the roughly chopped yellow onion, give a few pulses, and then return the carrots and beets to the food processor bowl, along with ½ cup (75 g) roasted sunflower seeds, ½ cup (50 g) toasted walnuts, a handful of fresh cilantro leaves, 1 tablespoon soy sauce, 2 large chipotle chiles (or 1 teaspoon chipotle chile powder), 1½ teaspoons kosher salt, and flaxseed egg. Pulse until combined— about 2 minutes, scraping down the sides as needed. Some texture should still remain, but the mixture should hold together. Refrigerate the mixture until ready to use, or shape into 6 patties and freeze in a single layer on a lined baking sheet, and then transfer to freezer bags to use anytime!

(Continued)

Prep the fries: Preheat the oven to 425°F (220°C) with the racks in the upper and lower third position. Cut 2 medium sweet potatoes into ½-inch-thick (12 mm) wedges, trying to make the pieces as even as possible—this will help them all get crispy! Transfer the wedges to the lined baking sheets. Drizzle with about 2 tablespoons olive oil and sprinkle 1 tablespoon cornstarch over the two pans. Season with a generous amount of flaky salt and toss until the wedges are evenly coated.

Cook the fries: Bake for 20 minutes, and then flip the fries and rotate the pans in case there are any hot spots in your oven. Bake for 15 to 18 more minutes, keeping a close eye on them during this second round to avoid burning. When they are deep golden brown, transfer the fries all to one tray, spreading them out in a single layer so they retain their crispness, and reuse the other tray for the burgers.

Meanwhile, cook the burgers: Brush the empty parchment-lined sheet you used to cook the fries with a little bit of olive oil. Form the burger meat into patties if you haven't already, place on the tray, and bake for 15 minutes, then flip the burgers and cook 10 minutes more, until both sides are golden and the patties are firm. Return the fries to the oven for the last few minutes of baking to warm.

Assemble and serve: Serve the burgers on seeded bread or buns with avocado crema, sliced red onion, and sprouts. I like to serve extra crema on the side for dipping the fries!

Red Lentil, Carrot, and Enoki Mushroom Stew

Serves 4 to 6 as a meal

Enoki are truly the mellowest of mushrooms; they are tender, delicate, and their flavor is mild and nutty and just a little sweet. They almost melt away completely into this stew, but throwing them in at the end imparts something very special and turned this sleeper into a hit at home. If you don't have smoked soy sauce, substitute regular soy sauce and ½ teaspoon smoked paprika for the same smoky flavor.

PRODUCE
1 onion
6 large carrots (11 ounces/325 g)
3 cloves garlic, sliced
7 ounces (200 g) fresh enoki mushrooms

DAIRY
Unsweetened plain or coconut yogurt (optional),
  for serving

PANTRY
Extra-virgin olive oil
Kosher salt and freshly ground black pepper
2½ cups (1 pound/454 g) red lentils
8 cups (2 liters) vegetable or mushroom stock
2 tablespoons mushroom powder (see page 29)
2 tablespoons smoked soy sauce (see page 29)

Prep the produce: Chop the onion, and thinly slice 6 carrots about ¼ inch (6 mm) thick on a bit of an angle. Thinly slice 3 cloves garlic. Trim the ends of the enoki mushrooms.

Cook the stew: In a large pot, heat a few tablespoons olive oil over medium-high heat. Once the oil is shimmering, add the onions and carrots. Cook until the onions are soft and translucent, about 7 minutes. Add the garlic and cook until fragrant, about 2 minutes. Season well with salt and pepper.

Add 2½ cups (454 g) red lentils and 8 cups (2 liters) stock. Cook, partially covered, until the lentils are extremely tender, about 25 minutes.

Add 7 ounces (200 g) fresh enoki mushrooms, 2 tablespoons mushroom powder, and 2 tablespoons smoked soy sauce.

Finish and serve: Cook just until the mushrooms have softened, about 2 minutes. Season to taste with more salt and pepper. Serve with a little yogurt if you wish! Store in an airtight container in the fridge for up to 4 days, or in the freezer for up to 3 months.

Health Nut

Black Bean Tostadas with Avocado and Crispy Leeks

Makes 16 (serves 4 as a meal)

These tostadas remind me of my friend Jason because we like to eat bean tostadas together at this amazing little place in Bed-Stuy called For All Things Good. He never likes to go out to eat because basically all he eats is beans, but he'll meet me there. These refried beans are delicious enough to eat on their own. I love keeping them around for little breakfast tacos with scrambled eggs and avocado too.

....

PRODUCE
4 cloves garlic
1 bunch fresh cilantro
2 oranges
2 avocados
1 recipe Crispy Leeks (page 265; reserve the greens to cook with the beans)
Lime wedges, for serving

PANTRY
1 pound (450 g) dried black beans
2 bay leaves
Kosher salt
16 corn tortillas
Avocado oil, for brushing
Salsa Macha (page 276)

Prep the beans: Soak 1 pound (450 g) black beans in cold water to cover for at least 8 hours or overnight. Smash and peel 4 cloves garlic and trim the stems from 1 bunch cilantro, reserving the stems and leaves.

Cook the beans: Add the greens of the leeks, garlic, cilantro stems, and 2 bay leaves to a large stockpot along with the rinsed and drained beans and 14 cups (3.3 liters) fresh water. Bring to a boil and simmer uncovered until the beans are tender. This can take anywhere from 2 to 4 hours. Remove the tough leek

greens and bay leaves. At this point, you can go on to make the refried beans, or store the beans in an airtight containers in the fridge or freezer to use another day.

Make the refried beans: Add 6 cups (1.2 kg) of the reserved beans and their liquid to the pan (this works out to about 4 cups/685 g of beans and 2 cups/475 ml liquid). Mash the beans up with a potato masher, a spoon, or anything else you've got that can get those beans nice and smooth. Cook, stirring occasionally, until the beans create a nice paste, similar to mashed potatoes, and are cooked through. Add the freshly squeezed juice from 2 oranges and season to taste with salt.

Bake the tostadas: Preheat the oven to 400°F (205°C) with the rack in the center. Place 6 corn tortillas on a rimmed baking sheet and brush with oil. Flip and brush the other side. Bake until crispy, 20 to 25 minutes.

Assemble and serve: Slice the avocados. Spread some of the beans onto each tostada. Top with sliced avocado, salsa macha, and crispy leeks. Garnish with fresh cilantro leaves and a lime wedge.

Brothy White Beans with Parm and Pesto

Serves 2 as a light meal

These are delicious on their own, or with some greens swirled into them. Try them with a crunchy piece of sourdough or over some farro or other nutty grain. Parmesan gives the beans a savoriness and funky depth of flavor that makes it hard to believe they are vegetarian.

PRODUCE
5 cloves garlic
1 lemon

DAIRY
Wedge Parmesan, with rind

PANTRY
1 cup (205 g) dried white beans, such as cannellini
Extra-virgin olive oil
8 cups (2 liters) chicken stock, store-bought or homemade (page 265), or water
2 bay leaves
Kosher salt and freshly ground black pepper
Pistachio Pesto (page 274), for serving

Prep the beans: Cover 1 cup (205 g) white beans with water by at least 2 inches (5 cm). Soak for 8 hours or up to overnight. Drain.

Cook the beans: In a large heavy-bottomed pot, heat a good glug of oil over medium. Peel and thinly slice 5 cloves garlic and add to the pot. Cook until just golden brown, about 2 minutes.

Add 8 cups (2 liters) chicken stock or water, 2 bay leaves, the Parmesan rind, the soaked beans, and zest of 1 lemon and bring to a boil. Reduce the heat to a simmer and cook, covered, until the beans are tender, about 75 minutes. Taste and season with salt and pepper. Remove the Parmesan rind and bay leaves.

Assemble and serve: Swirl in a bit of pistachio pesto and grate Parmesan over the top. Store the beans and their broth in an airtight container for up to 4 days in the fridge or 3 months in the freezer.

Butter Beans with Chile Tomato Saffron Broth

Serves 4 as a light meal

Nick Curtola from the Four Horsemen in Brooklyn makes butter beans that I dream about. They aren't on the menu all the time, and now I live in LA, so I've had to figure out how to make something sort of like them on my own. Butter beans are creamy and luscious, and this saffron-painted broth is like liquid gold. I like to make big batches when Sungolds are in season and keep them in my freezer for cooler days. I serve them with a little dollop of labneh and a crusty piece of bread.

PRODUCE
1 yellow onion
2 cloves garlic
1 Fresno chile
2 pints (570 g) Sungolds or other sweet cherry tomatoes

PANTRY
Extra-virgin olive oil
1 cup (170 g) dried butter beans
Pinch saffron
8 cups (2 liters) chicken stock, store-bought or homemade (page 265)
Kosher salt and freshly ground black pepper

Prep the aromatics: Peel the onion, cut it in half, and thinly slice.

Cook the beans: Add a little bit of olive oil to a large heavy-bottomed pot and heat over medium-high. Add the onions and let cook, stirring occasionally, until completely soft and translucent, about 7 minutes. Thinly slice 2 cloves garlic and the Fresno chile and add to the pot, and cook another minute or so, just until they are both fragrant. Add the beans, 1 pint (285 g) cherry tomatoes, a pinch of saffron, and 8 cups (2 liters) stock. Bring to a boil, and then reduce to a simmer. Cover and simmer for about 2 hours, occasionally checking for tenderness.

Once the beans are tender, add the remaining 1 pint (285 g) cherry tomatoes, and begin seasoning with salt and pepper. Continue to cook, uncovered, until the tomatoes begin to break down but still retain some texture and the beans are completely soft, about 45 minutes more.

Serve or store: You can enjoy these immediately or store in an airtight container in the refrigerator for up to 4 days or in the freezer for up to 6 months.

Lentil Loaf

Serves 6 to 8

Maybe a lentil loaf doesn't sound that thrilling, but you haven't had this one yet. It has so much flavor and texture, I think it's more satisfying than a real meatloaf. Even carnivores will ask for a second slice.

....

PRODUCE
3 medium carrots (about 10½ ounces/300 g)
1 large yellow onion
2 stalks celery
5 cloves garlic
8 ounces (240 g) cremini mushrooms
1 cup (30 g) loosely packed fresh parsley
2 cups (400 g) brown lentils

PROTEIN
3 large eggs

PANTRY
1 cup (100 g) walnuts
3 bay leaves
Extra-virgin olive oil
1 (4 to 6-ounce/115 g) can tomato paste
¾ cup (45 g) nutritional yeast
½ cup (30 g) panko breadcrumbs
Kosher salt and freshly ground black pepper
¼ cup smoked soy sauce
2 tablespoons apple cider vinegar
2 tablespoons maple syrup
¼ teaspoon cayenne pepper

Prep the loaf: Preheat the oven to 425°F (220°C) with the rack in the center position. Toast the walnuts until golden brown, about 8 minutes. Chop 3 medium carrots, 1 large onion, 2 celery stalks, and 3 cloves garlic and thinly slice 8 ounces (240 g) cremini mushrooms and set aside while you cook the lentils. Peel the remaining 2 cloves garlic. Add the lentils and 8 cups (2 liters) water to a medium pot, along with the remaining whole cloves garlic and 3 bay leaves. Bring to a boil and then reduce the heat to a simmer for about

25 minutes, until the lentils have just a little tooth to them. Drain any liquid and transfer the lentils to a large bowl, removing the bay leaves and garlic cloves.

Cook the aromatics: Return your medium pot to the stove over medium heat. Add ¼ cup (60 ml) olive oil and sauté the carrots, onion, celery, and chopped garlic until just tender, about 6 minutes. Add 3 tablespoons tomato paste, cook down for a minute or two, then add the mushrooms. Cook the veggies until most of the mushroom liquid is absorbed, about 6 minutes.

Make the loaf mixture: Add the vegetable mixture and all but 1 cup (200 g) of the cooked lentils to a food processor, and pulse until combined but not mushy. Mix in the remaining lentils, the toasted walnuts, 1 cup (30 g) fresh parsley, ¾ cup (45 g) nutritional yeast, ½ cup (30 g) breadcrumbs, 3 large eggs, 4 teaspoons kosher salt, and 1 teaspoon pepper.

Make the glaze: In a small bowl, mix the remaining 4 tablespoons (60 ml) tomato paste, 2 tablespoons smoked soy sauce, 2 tablespoons vinegar, 2 tablespoons maple syrup, and ¼ teaspoon cayenne.

Bake and serve: Line a 9 by 5-inch (23 by 12 cm) loaf pan with parchment paper, leaving overhang on two sides so you can lift it out, and set it on a baking sheet to catch drips. Brush the parchment with a little oil. Add the loaf to the pan, brush with the glaze, cover the pan with foil, and cook for 50 minutes. Uncover and cook for 10 to 15 minutes, until the glaze begins to brown in spots.

Let the loaf rest 15 minutes before serving. Leftovers can be wrapped in foil and stored in the fridge for up to 4 days or frozen for up to 3 months.

Kitchari with Cilantro Chutney

Serves 12 as a light meal

If ever you've been to an ashram, than you are familiar with kitchari. An ancient Ayurvedic cleansing meal, it's a warming combination of spiced yellow mung beans, which can be found in Indian markets and online, and rice meant to balance your doshas, but it's also extremely nourishing, and easy on the body, and simple to make. Oh, and it's delicious. Add some chutney, a swirl of yogurt, or just some fresh cilantro to provide a little texture and a burst of bright flavor and enjoy.

PRODUCE
1-inch (2.5 cm) piece fresh ginger

PANTRY
1 cup (165 g) white basmati rice
2 cups (395 g) yellow moong (mung) dal
2 tablespoons ghee or coconut oil
1 teaspoon whole cumin seeds
1 teaspoon whole mustard seeds
1 teaspoon ground coriander seeds
Cilantro Chutney (optional, page 273) or fresh
  cilantro sprigs, for serving

DAIRY
Unsweetened plain or coconut yogurt, for serving

Prep the ingredients: In a large bowl, combine 1 cup (165 g) basmati rice and 2 cups (395 g) yellow moong dal and let soak for 20 minutes. Drain and rinse well, until the water runs clear.

Peel a 1-inch (2.5 cm) piece fresh ginger. Grate using a Microplane or finely mince.

Start cooking: Meanwhile in a large pot, heat 2 tablespoons ghee over medium heat. Add 1 teaspoon cumin seeds, 1 teaspoon mustard seeds, 1 teaspoon coriander seeds, and the ginger and cook until just fragrant, about 1 minute, being careful not to burn them.

Add the rice and dal and 10 cups (2.35 liters) water. Bring to a boil and then reduce the heat to a simmer, with the lid partially covering the pot. Stir occasionally and cook until most of the water is absorbed and the rice and dal are very tender, about 1 hour.

Serve: Top with a dollop of yogurt and a bit of cilantro chutney or fresh cilantro, if desired.

Fava Bean Puree with Bitter Greens

Serves 6 to 10 as a starter

I used to live on DeKalb Avenue in Bed-Stuy and would walk over to Fort Greene to the Italian restaurant Roman's; it's one of the experiences I miss the most about Brooklyn. It was the best in the summer, in the evening, just as the sun was setting, without a jacket on. Cool breeze, loud sidewalks . . . Walking through those doors into that dimly lit, just-right little space, where you could depend on knowing someone at least one table or at the bar. Knowing you'll order everything, even that second bottle of wine, but first . . . the fava puree. Bob's Red Mill produces already shelled dried fava beans, available online if your local grocery doesn't stock their products—beans without their shells have the best flavor.

PRODUCE
½ small yellow onion
1 head, plus 3 cloves garlic
1 bunch (8 to 10 ounces/280 g) dandelion greens
  or other bitter greens
1 lemon

PANTRY
1 cup (175 g) dried shelled, blanched fava beans
7 tablespoons extra-virgin olive oil, plus more for
  drizzling
Kosher salt
1 teaspoon crushed red pepper
Sourdough bread, for serving

Cook the beans: Add 1 cup (175 g) dried favas to a large pot along with the ½ onion. Cut 1 head of garlic in half crosswise and add to the pot, skins and all. Cover the favas with 3 cups (710 ml) water. Bring to a boil, reduce the heat to a simmer, and cover and cook until tender, about 1 hour (this will depend on the freshness of the beans).

Make the puree: Remove the onion and garlic halves from the favas and discard. Drain the favas and transfer to a food processor. Puree a bit before drizzling in 2 tablespoons olive oil. Continue to process until the puree is incredibly smooth, about 2 minutes. Season with salt to taste and then pulse again.

Cook the greens: Slice 3 cloves garlic. Prepare an ice bath. Bring a 4-quart (3.75 liter) pot of heavily salted water to a boil. Add 10 ounces (280 g) dandelion greens and cook until tender, about 1 to 2 minutes. Set greens in the ice bath, and once cool, remove and squeeze out the water with your hands. Roughly chop and set aside until ready to assemble.

In the same pot, combine a few tablespoons of olive oil, the sliced garlic, and 1 teaspoon crushed red pepper. Cook until fragrant, about 1 minute. Add the reserved greens and cook until they are warmed through, about 2 minutes. Season to taste with salt.

Assemble and serve: Spoon the puree into a serving dish, spoon the greens in the center, and drizzle with plenty of olive oil. Offer sourdough bread alongside.

Very Good Vegan Chili

Serves 6 as a meal

My friend Glennis has a specialty dish she calls double beans. I tease her about it, but before I taught her all I could about cooking during COVID—it was truly all she would make. So this is a new recipe to get into Glennis's (and your!) rotation, not just a double-bean but a triple-bean chili, full of "it's been simmering on the stove all day" flavor, in minutes. Blending a bit of the chili helps the beans break down a bit and release their starches, making it feel really rich and hearty. Don't skip out on the cornbread on page 263, slathered with Miso Tahini Butter (page 273).

....

PRODUCE
1 yellow onion
2 cloves garlic
3 medium carrots
Fresh cilantro, for serving
Limes, for serving

DAIRY
Unsweetened plain or coconut yogurt, for serving

PANTRY
Extra-virgin olive oil
1 teaspoon ground cumin
1 teaspoon ground coriander
2 tablespoons ancho chile powder
1 tablespoon smoked paprika
1 teaspoon dried Mexican oregano
2 tablespoons tomato paste
2 (14-ounce/400 g) cans black beans
1 (14-ounce/400 g) can kidney beans
1 (14-ounce/400 g) can pinto beans
1 (28-ounce/795 g) can fire-roasted diced
   tomatoes
Kosher salt
Masa Harina Cornbread (page 263), for serving
Miso Tahini Butter (page 273), for serving

Prep and cook: Slice an onion and 2 cloves garlic and chop 3 medium carrots. Heat a large heavy-bottomed pot over medium-high. Add a good glug of oil. Add the veggies to the pot. Cook until the onions are soft and translucent, about 7 to 9 minutes, stirring to keep anything from browning. Add 1 teaspoon ground cumin, 1 teaspoon ground coriander, 2 tablespoons ancho chile powder, 1 tablespoon smoked paprika, and 1 teaspoon oregano. Give it a minute, and then add 2 tablespoons tomato paste. Cook another 2 minutes. Drain two 14-ounce (400 g) cans black beans, one 14-ounce (400 g) can kidney beans, and one 14-ounce (400 g) can pinto beans. Add all the beans to the pot along with one 28-ounce (795 g) can fire-roasted diced tomatoes with its juices.

Bring to a boil, and then let simmer, partially covered, for 25 minutes, stirring occasionally.

Use an immersion blender to puree a bit of the bean mixture to create a smoother, richer consistency, or carefully add a couple of ladlesful of the chili into a blender and blend for the same effect. Season with salt.

Assemble and serve: Serve topped with yogurt, fresh cilantro, and with lime wedges and cornbread (you should really make my masa harina cornbread and a little of the miso tahini butter, okay?). Store the leftover chili in an airtight container in the fridge for 4 days or in the freezer for up to 3 months.

Escarole and White Bean Soup with Lots of Lemon

Serves 6 as a meal

Affectionately known as "Beans and Greens" in this house, this one is delicious without the little meatballs, but they do make it a bit heartier if you do eat meat! I love this soup because it is SO quick and easy to make and is a great way to use up any handfuls of wilting greens you may have in the garden or fridge, but escarole is my favorite. My friend Benny sometimes likes to add orzo and handfuls of herbs too.

PRODUCE
1 onion
3 cloves garlic
1 head escarole, leaves separated
2 lemons

DAIRY
¼ cup (15 g) grated Parmesan cheese
3- to 4-inch (7.5 to 10 cm) piece Parmesan rind

MEAT
1 pound (450 g) ground chicken thighs

PANTRY
Kosher salt and freshly ground black pepper
¼ teaspoon crushed red pepper flakes
½ teaspoon fennel seeds, toasted
¼ cup (45 g) panko breadcrumbs
Extra-virgin olive oil
8 cups (2 liters) chicken stock, store-bought or homemade (page 265)
4 cups (430 g) cooked white beans (page 92) or 2 (14-ounce/400 g) cans

Make the meatballs: In a medium bowl, combine 1 pound (450 g) ground chicken thighs, 1 teaspoon kosher salt, pepper to taste, ¼ teaspoon red pepper flakes, ½ teaspoon toasted fennel seeds, ¼ cup (15 g) grated Parmesan, and ¼ cup (45 g) breadcrumbs. Mix well and use a tablespoon measure to make even-sized scoops.

Cook the meatballs: Heat a large stockpot over medium-high heat. Add a couple tablespoons of olive oil, and once it's simmering add the meatballs. Cook until brown on all sides, about 8 minutes. Remove from pot and set on a plate.

Prep the aromatics and make the soup: Thinly slice 1 onion and 3 cloves garlic. Add a little drizzle of oil to a large pot and heat over medium-high. Add the onion and cook until soft and translucent, about 6 minutes. Add the garlic and cook just until fragrant, about 2 minutes more. Add 8 cups (2 liters) stock and the Parmesan rind and bring to a simmer. Add 4 cups (430 g) homemade white beans or two 14-ounce (400 g) cans and the meatballs and let simmer together until everything is warmed though, about 10 minutes. Season with salt and pepper to taste, and then add the escarole. Cook until wilted. Stir in a big squeeze of lemon juice and check the seasoning again.

Garnish and serve: Serve each bowl with lemon wedges and a bit of grated Parmesan.

SOUPS & GRAIN BOWLS

A bowl is just a vessel.

It's a circle.

And a hug, right? It's sort of like a hug the way everything
is fit snugly inside. And it can hold you—everything you need
for a whole meal is right there.

I think a bowl is its own food group.

My comfort foods come in bowls. Healthy grains and beans
and veggies, complete meals that can be made ahead
and enjoyed all week or to feed a table of friends and family.

Soups to nourish you. Fresh, light, quenching bowlfuls for
warm days and savory stews and broths to warm you from
the inside on cool days.

An embrace, a squeeze, a cuddle. Bowls filled to the brim.

Carrot Ginger Saffron Soup with Rosey Harissa

Serves 4 as a light meal or starter

I grow a whole garden row of carrots every year, with plans to enjoy them in things like this simple velvety soup. But Snax, my dog, loves carrots, sneaks into the beds to pull them out, and eats most of them before I've ever had a chance to cook with them. But even if I have to buy the carrots, I still make this soup—the saffron tints it even more golden and gives it just a little something special. I love to top it with my Rosey Harissa (page 274), but yogurt and a bit of pistachios or pistachio butter (page 266) swirled in would be delicious (and decadent!) too. Double this recipe for a crowd or a bigger batch to freeze.

PRODUCE
1 pound (454 g) carrots
½ yellow onion
2-inch (5 cm) piece fresh ginger
2 cloves garlic

PANTRY
Extra-virgin olive oil
Pinch saffron
**4 cups (945 ml) water or vegetable stock
   (page 265), plus more if needed**
Kosher salt and freshly ground black pepper
Rosey Harissa (page 274), for serving
Nut Butter (preferably pistachio; page 266)

Prep the produce: Peel and dice 1 pound (454 g) carrots and ½ onion. Peel and mince 2 inches (5 cm) ginger. Crush 2 cloves garlic.

Make the soup: Heat a good glug of olive oil in a large heavy-bottomed pot over medium heat. Add the carrots, onion, and garlic. Cook until very soft and the onions are translucent, about 10 minutes. Add 1 pinch saffron and 4 cups (945 ml) water or stock. Bring to a boil. Reduce the heat to a simmer and cook until everything is very soft, about 25 minutes.

Finish and serve: Use an immersion blender to blend the veggies and broth into a smooth puree, or carefully transfer the mixture to a blender in batches and blend. Once the soup is smooth, adjust the consistency if desired by adding a bit more liquid. Season to taste with salt and pepper and serve with the rosey harissa (page 274) or a bit of pistachio butter (page 266).

Crispy Rice and Salmon Bowl with Quick Pickles and Greens

Serves 4 as a meal

Seasoned sushi rice crisped to deep golden brown topped with plump little nuggets of perfectly spiced salmon, with a big pile of green veggies—to me, this is the perfect meal. It works even better with leftover cooked rice—so use that if you have it on hand, or make sure you give yourself enough time to chill the freshly cooked rice in the fridge before crisping it!

PRODUCE
2 Japanese or English cucumbers
2 handfuls loosely packed dark leafy greens, such as spinach
2 avocados

PROTEIN
1 pound (454 g) skinless salmon fillet, preferably wild

PANTRY
Kosher salt
¼ cup (60 ml) plus 2 tablespoons rice vinegar
4 cups (600 g) cooked short-grain sushi rice
Neutral oil, such as sunflower or avocado
¼ cup (60 ml) soy sauce
1 teaspoon fish sauce
2 tablespoons (30 ml) honey
1 tablespoon (15 ml) chili sauce (such as Sambal)
1 teaspoon garlic powder
1 teaspoon togarashi
1 cup (160 g) frozen edamame, thawed
Furikake, for serving

Make the pickles: Smash 2 cucumbers and slice into ½-inch (12 mm) chunks. Add to a colander or fine-mesh strainer set over a bowl and sprinkle with a generous amount of salt. Let sit for 20 minutes. Transfer to a bowl and toss with ¼ cup (60 ml) rice vinegar. Let sit at least 10 minutes, or up to a week or two in the fridge.

Meanwhile, make the crispy rice: Fluff the warm, cooked rice with a fork and add 2 tablespoons rice vinegar and salt.

Line an 8-inch (20 cm) square baking dish with parchment paper, and then add the rice. Squish down into a solid layer using your hands or a measuring cup. Refrigerate for at least 2 hours but overnight is best.

Cut into eight 4-inch by 2-inch (10 by 5 cm) rectangles. Heat a little bit of neutral oil in a nonstick or cast-iron pan over medium-high heat. Add the rice squares and cook until golden brown, about 10 minutes. Flip carefully and cook 10 minutes more. Sprinkle with a bit of salt.

Make the dipping sauce: In a small bowl, combine ¼ cup (60 ml) soy sauce, 1 teaspoon fish sauce,

(Continued)

2 tablespoons (30 ml) honey, and 1 tablespoon (15 ml) chili sauce and whisk to blend

Prepare and cook the salmon: Cut the salmon into 2-inch (5 cm) pieces. In a large bowl, add the salmon and sprinkle with 1 teaspoon garlic powder, salt, and 1 teaspoon togarashi and toss to combine.

Add about 1 tablespoon neutral oil to the pan that you cooked the rice in and heat over medium high. Add the salmon, and let cook, undisturbed, for 2 to 3 minutes. Begin to flip the pieces when they easily come off the pan, about 2 minutes. When the fish is opaque throughout, about 10 minutes, transfer to a plate and wipe out the pan.

Cook the veggies: Add the spinach and edamame to the pan with ¼ cup (60 ml) water. Turn the heat to medium high, season with salt, and cook, stirring occasionally, until the spinach has wilted and the water has evaporated.

Assemble and serve: In each serving bowl, put 1 crispy rice square and top it with salmon pieces, some spinach and edamame, pickles, avocado slices, and plenty of furikake. Serve with the sauce on the side.

Parsnip and Potato Soup with Crispy Leeks

Serves 4 to 6 as a light meal or starter

Parsnips, in my humble opinion, are at the top of the list when it comes to fall vegetables, but I think they are extremely underrated. They have an incredible, complex flavor. Roasting them gives them a little bit of extra toasty-ness, and I let it shine in this soup! It's deeply warming for the coldest fall and winter days. For even more nuttiness, try adding some toasted kasha on top.

PRODUCE
1 pound (454 g) parsnips
1 head garlic
4 leeks
3 medium Yukon gold potatoes (about 1 pound/ 454 g)
1 recipe Parsley Oil (page 269)

PANTRY
Extra-virgin olive oil
Kosher salt and freshly ground black pepper
6 cups (1.4 liters) vegetable stock
1 cup (240 ml) water, coconut milk, or other nut milk, store-bought or homemade (page 266)

Prep the produce: Preheat the oven to 425°F (220°C). Peel and chop 1 pound (454 g) parsnips into 1-inch (2.5 cm) pieces. Line a baking sheet with parchment paper. Cut off the top one-third of 1 head garlic. Drizzle with a bit of olive oil and wrap in a small piece of parchment-lined foil.

Roast the parsnips and garlic: Toss the parsnips with 1 tablespoon olive oil and season with a generous amount of salt and pepper. Spread the parsnips out in a single layer on the prepared baking sheet and place in the preheated oven, along with the foil-wrapped garlic clove. Roast until the parsnips are golden brown and tender, about 20 minutes, and remove from the oven.

The garlic will take a little longer, but you can start getting everything else going while it continues to roast, about 25 minutes more.

Meanwhile, make the crispy leeks: Follow the recipe on page 265, but reserve half the thinly sliced leeks for the soup.

Cook the soup: Add the reserved leeks to a large pot with a little olive oil and cook over medium-high heat until soft and translucent, about 9 minutes.

Peel 1 pound (454 g) Yukon gold potatoes and cut into 1-inch (2.5 cm) pieces. Add the potatoes and 6 cups (1.4 liters) vegetable stock to the pot with the softened leeks. Add the roasted parsnips and garlic and bring everything to a boil. Reduce to a simmer and cook until the vegetables are very tender, about 25 to 30 minutes. Turn off the heat.

Finish and serve: Using an immersion blender, carefully puree the soup until creamy and smooth (or wait for the soup to cool a bit and puree in batches in a regular blender). Season with salt and pepper and adjust the thickness of the soup with 1 cup (235 ml) water or cashew or coconut milk, as needed. Top with parsley oil and crispy leeks before serving. Store any leftovers in an airtight container for up to 4 days, or freeze for up to 3 months.

Turmeric Ginger Bone Broth

Makes 4 quarts (3.75 liters)

Bone broth is so easy and it makes a huge batch so there is plenty to freeze and have on hand for sick days. I like to have it in addition to a salad or light meal sometimes, because it makes me feel more full, or just sip it on cold days. Bone broth is full of collagen, vitamins, and minerals, and is great for gut health.

PRODUCE
2 carrots
2 celery stalks
1 onion
4 cloves garlic
2-inch (5 cm) piece turmeric, or 2 teaspoons ground turmeric
2-inch (5 cm) piece ginger

PROTEIN
2 pounds (900 g) chicken wings or feet

PANTRY
2 bay leaves
½ teaspoon black peppercorns
2 tablespoons apple cider vinegar
Himalayan or sea salt

Prep the produce: Chop 2 carrots and 2 celery stalks into two or three pieces. Leave skin on the onion and cut it in half. Crush 4 cloves garlic. Thinly slice the turmeric and ginger (it's okay to leave the skin on).

Cook on the stove: Add everything to a large stock pot and add 4 to 6 quarts (4 to 6 liters) water, enough to cover everything. Bring to a boil and then reduce to a simmer. Cover with a lid, and keep at a low simmer for 12 to 24 hours. The longer you cook it the more collagen, vitamins, and minerals are able to be extracted from the bones. The slow cooker is a great option if you're unable to be around to keep an eye on the stovetop for such a long time.

Or cook in a slow cooker: Set the slow cooker to low, and cook for 12 to 24 hours. This might mean resetting the timer a couple of times!

Strain and serve: Carefully strain the broth though a fine-mesh sieve or cheesecloth and discard all the solids. Season the broth with sea salt and either serve or transfer to jars with tight-fitting lids. Keep in the fridge for up to 5 days or freeze for up to 6 months.

Chilled Zucchini Cilantro Soup with Yogurt and Breadcrumbs

Serves 4 to 6 as a light meal or starter

I only came around to chilled soups fairly recently, but now I feel like I've been missing out on so much my whole life. This soup couldn't be easier to make, and it feels so clean and healthy—but it really has a lot of flavor. It's a great lunch or summer starter.

PRODUCE
4 medium zucchini (about 2 pounds/900 g)
1 white onion
1 bunch fresh cilantro
1 lemon
Coriander or cilantro blossoms (optional)

DAIRY
**½ cup (120 ml) unsweetened plain or coconut
  yogurt, for serving**

PANTRY
Extra-virgin olive oil
Kosher salt and freshly ground black pepper
**4 cups (945 liters) water or vegetable stock
  (page 265)**
½ cup (25 g) Basic Breadcrumbs (page 265)

Prep the produce: Fill a small pot with water and bring to a boil. Fill a large bowl with ice water. Cut 4 medium zucchini into ¼-inch-thick (6 mm) half-moons. Peel and chop 1 onion. Trim off and discard the thick stems from 1 bunch cilantro, blanch the remaining sprigs quickly (about 30 seconds) in the boiling water, and use tongs to transfer to the ice bath.

Make the soup: Add a generous drizzle of olive oil to a Dutch oven or other medium to large pot or deep straight-sided skillet. Add the onion to the pot. Cook, until soft and translucent, about 8 minutes. Season with salt and pepper. Add the zucchini. Cook until the zucchini is beginning to soften, about 6 minutes. Add 4 cups (945 ml) vegetable stock or water to the pot and bring to a simmer.

Simmer until the zucchini is very tender, about 15 minutes. Let the soup cool until it is safe to blend without burning yourself, then transfer to a blender along with cilantro. Add ¼ cup (60 ml) olive oil and blend until the soup is velvety smooth. Taste and adjust the seasoning. Finish with a little squeeze of lemon juice to taste. Refrigerate until chilled completely, about 2 hours or up to overnight.

Fry the breadcrumbs and serve: Heat a small skillet over medium-high. Add about 2 tablespoons of olive oil and the breadcrumbs. Cook, stirring, until golden brown and toasty, about 5 minutes. Season with salt.

Serve the chilled soup with a dollop of yogurt and some olive oil–fried breadcrumbs and cilantro or coriander blossoms and a good amount of lemon zest.

Tomato and Melon Gazpacho

Serves 4 to 6 as a light meal or starter

I am melon-obsessed in the summer, and that's probably why I've never liked a gazpacho as much as I like this one. Serve as cold as humanly possible. Let it sit overnight for maximum flavor. If you don't have pickled Fresno chiles ready to go, substitute fresh Fresno chiles and add some apple cider vinegar, 1 tablespoon at a time, until the desired tanginess is reached. No Fresno chiles? Jalapeños or serranos are fine, but the Fresno has a special fruitiness that is worth seeking out. They can usually be found at Whole Foods.

PRODUCE

1 small (about 6 pounds/2.7 kg) seedless red watermelon

2 big fat juicy red heirloom tomatoes

1 English cucumber

2 tablespoons pickled sliced Fresno chiles, or more to taste

Coriander blossoms, basil, or just some pretty cilantro, for serving

PANTRY

Kosher salt

⅓ cup (75 ml) really good extra-virgin olive oil

Prep the produce: Remove the rind from a 6-pound (2.7 kg) watermelon and cut the melon into 2-inch (5 cm) cubes. You should have about 3 cups (450 g) melon cubes. Core 2 big heirloom tomatoes and remove the seeds. Peel 1 English cucumber and cut into 2-inch (5 cm) pieces.

Blend and chill: Put the watermelon, tomatoes, cucumber, and 2 tablespoons pickled Fresno chile slices into a blender and blend until velvety smooth. Taste for seasoning and salt as needed. Refrigerate for at least 4 hours, or up to overnight.

Garnish and serve: Add a swirl of oil on the gazpacho and top with cilantro, basil, or edible flowers, then enjoy immediately.

Roasted Shiitake Soup with Crispy Tofu

Serves 4 as a meal

This is a soup I make for myself very often. The brown rice and tofu make it hearty, but it's loaded with greens and shiitakes, so it's very healthy too. The broth is extremely flavorful and warming, with lots of soothing ginger. This is a perfect sick-day soup. It's a bit of a project, because it has a few components, but they are all fairly simple so it's kind of relaxing. It makes a big batch, so you'll have plenty to share or to take you through the week. I have never recommended warm avocado in any other dish but this one. It somehow just works!

....

PRODUCE
1 pound (454 g) shiitake mushrooms
1 bunch dark leafy greens (14 ounce/400 g), such as Swiss chard
1 avocado (optional), sliced, for serving

PROTEIN
2 (14-ounce/397 g) blocks extra-firm tofu

PANTRY
Neutral oil, such as sunflower or avocado
¼ cup (60 ml) soy sauce
Kosher salt
1 recipe Umami Mushroom Stock (page 270)
2 cups (380 g) cooked brown rice (see page 268)
Togarashi, for serving

Prep the tofu and produce: Preheat the oven to 425°F (220°C). Press two 14-ounce (397 g) blocks tofu in a tofu press or cut each block lengthwise into five pieces and press using paper towels or clean dish towels and a heavy pan for at least 20 minutes. Cut into 1-inch (2.5 cm) cubes.

Thinly slice 1 pound (454 g) shiitake mushrooms. Remove thick stems from 1 bunch of leafy greens. Tear into bite-size pieces. Wash thoroughly and set aside (there's no need to dry it).

Roast the mushrooms and tofu: Line two rimmed baking sheets with parchment paper. To one baking sheet, add the sliced shiitakes, a little drizzle neutral oil, and ¼ cup (60 ml) soy sauce. Bake until the moisture is absorbed but the mushrooms are not completely dry, about 20 minutes.

In a large bowl, toss the tofu with a good drizzle of neutral oil and a generous sprinkle of salt. Add the tofu to the second prepared baking sheet in a single layer. Bake until golden brown and crispy, flipping halfway through, about 30 minutes.

Simmer the soup: In a large pot, bring 1 recipe umami mushroom stock to a gentle simmer, and before serving, stir in the leafy greens and cook until they are just wilted, about 5 minutes.

Assemble and serve: I like to fill each bowl with a little brown rice and then ladle the broth on top and add the crispy tofu like little croutons. Sprinkle each serving with togarashi. Serve with avocado slices as well, if desired. Store any leftover soup in an airtight container for up to 4 days, or freeze for up to 3 months.

Dragon Bowl

Serves 4 to 6 as a meal

The truth is, I could probably eat this every day for the rest of my life. A nod to one of my favorite vegan restaurants of all time (RIP Angelica Kitchen in the East Village), this macrobiotic meal hits every note for me. It's healthy, fulfilling, and is the flavor equivalent of a hippie, for sure. It seems like a lot of prep, but it also makes a big batch, so serve a group, or yourself, for several days.

PRODUCE
1 small kabocha squash (about 32 ounces/900 g)
1 (12-ounce/350 g) bunch curly kale

PROTEIN
1 (14-ounce/397 g) block extra-firm tofu

PANTRY
½ cup (10 g) "ready to use" or instant wakame
2 teaspoons plus 1 tablespoon toasted sesame oil
1 tablespoon plus 2 teaspoons ume vinegar
Kosher salt
1 tablespoon neutral oil, such as sunflower
  or avocado
4 cups (430 g) cooked white beans (see page 92)
  or 2 (14-ounce/400 g) cans
1 (6-inch/15 cm) piece kombu
¼ cup (60 ml) tahini
1 teaspoon white miso
Cooked brown rice (see page 268)
Gomasio (see page 28), for serving

Make the seaweed salad: Soak ½ cup (10 g) wakame in water to cover for about 10 minutes to soften. Drain and toss with 1 tablespoon sesame oil and 2 teaspoons ume vinegar, adding more oil or vinegar to taste.

Prep and cook the tofu: Preheat the oven to 425°F (220°C). Press one 14-ounce (397 g) block tofu using a tofu press or cut into 5 pieces lengthwise and press using paper towels or clean dish towels and a heavy pan. Once some of the moisture has been released,

season with a bit of salt. Cut into 1-inch (2.5 cm) pieces. Drizzle some neutral oil on a rimmed baking sheet, toss the tofu to coat, and roast, flipping once, until deep golden brown on all sides, about 25 minutes.

Prep the produce: Peel and remove the seeds from 1 small kabocha squash. Cut into 1-inch (2.5 cm) chunks. Remove the stems from 1 bunch kale.

Prep the beans: Add the beans to a medium pot with 1½ cups (360 ml) water and 1 piece kombu. Bring to a boil, and then simmer until the beans are soft and seasoned, about 20 minutes.

Cook the veggies: Set a steamer basket in a medium pot. Fill with water until it just about reaches the bottom of the basket. Add the kabocha and bring to a boil. Lower the heat to a simmer and cover. Cook until tender, 15 to 18 minutes, then remove and set aside. Add the kale to the steamer basket and cook until tender, about 3 minutes.

Make the miso tahini dressing: In a small bowl, whisk together ¼ cup (60 ml) tahini, 1 teaspoon miso, and 1 tablespoon ume vinegar. Whisk in 2 tablespoons warm water, adding more water by the teaspoon until you reach the desired consistency.

Assemble and serve: To assemble a bowl, put a big scoop of rice in the middle, and then add some seaweed salad, tofu, beans, kale, and squash around the sides. Drizzle with miso tahini dressing and season with gomasio.

Tuna, Avocado, and Grapefruit with Seed Crackers

Serves 2 as a meal

Of all the lunches I made for Martha, I will always distinctly remember the time she asked for tuna in olive oil, from a jar, half an avocado, sliced, and a supremed grapefruit. I thought about it for such a long time before making it for myself, which was many lost years, because it's really the easiest and most ideal midday meal. Serve with the Seed Crackers on page 270.

PRODUCE
1 grapefruit
1 avocado
1 lemon

PANTRY
1 (6.7-ounce/190 g) jar tuna in olive oil
Extra-virgin olive oil
Flaky salt and freshly ground black pepper
Seed Crackers (page 270)

Prep the produce: Using a small sharp knife or a serrated knife, remove the outer skin and pith from your grapefruit. Once just a ball of flesh remains, carefully cut a little V alongside each wedge of flesh to free just the juicy little jewels of fruit. Arrange the supremes on a plate (and make sure to squeeze and drink the juice from the remaining innards). Peel and slice the avocado. Cut the lemon into wedges.

Assemble and serve: Drain one 6.7-ounce (190 g) jar of tuna and arrange it and the avocado on the plate with the grapefruit. Drizzle it all with a bit of extra-virgin olive oil and sprinkle with flaky salt and pepper. Serve with the lemon wedges and seed crackers.

Lemony Chicken and Quinoa Bowl with Watercress, Cucumber, and Avocado

Serves 4 as a meal

This simple meal makes a perfect easy lunch or dinner. I like sprinkling a handful of herbs on top if I have fresh mint, dill, or chives on hand—and sometimes I crumble a bit of soft feta on top for a little extra something salty.

PRODUCE
3 cloves garlic
2 lemons
½ small shallot
1 (4-ounce/115 g) bunch watercress
1 English cucumber
1 avocado
Handful fresh mint

DAIRY
¼ cup (60 ml) unsweetened plain or coconut yogurt

PROTEIN
4 (6-ounce/115 g) boneless, skinless chicken breasts

PANTRY
½ cup (120 ml) extra-virgin olive oil
Kosher salt and freshly ground black pepper
1 teaspoon whole-grain mustard
1 teaspoon honey
2 cups (300 g) cooked quinoa (page 268)

Prep the chicken: On a plastic cutting board, cut four 6-ounce (115 g) chicken breasts into 1-inch (2.5 cm) pieces. In a large bowl, combine ¼ cup (60 ml) yogurt and ¼ cup (60 ml) olive oil. Grate 3 cloves garlic right into the bowl, followed by the zest of 1 lemon. Season generously with salt and pepper. Stir to combine. Let marinate for 15 minutes at room temperature or up to overnight in the refrigerator.

Roast the chicken: Preheat the oven to 425°F (220°C). Arrange the chicken on a baking sheet. Bake 15 minutes, toss, and bake for another 5 minutes, or until cooked through. Switch the oven to broil. Broil for 1 to 2 minutes, until the chicken chars on the edges.

Make the lemony vinaigrette: Peel and finely mince ½ shallot, then add to a small bowl or jar. Add the juice of 1 lemon, 1 teaspoon whole-grain mustard, ¼ cup (60 ml) extra-virgin olive oil, 1 teaspoon honey, and season generously with salt and pepper. Screw on the lid and give a good shake, or whisk to emulsify.

Assemble and serve: Trim 1 bunch watercress from its root if still attached. Cut 1 cucumber into ¼-inch (6 mm) half-moons or slices. Peel and slice 1 avocado. Arrange the quinoa in a bowl, topped with the chicken. Snuggle in the watercress and cucumbers and avocado. Serve drizzled with vinaigrette, fresh mint, and with additional lemon wedges on the side.

Spicy Peanut and Veggie Noodle Bowl

Serves 4 to 6 as a meal

This easy noodle bowl comes together in minutes and is super adaptable to whatever raw or leftover cooked veggies you have on hand, so feel free to mix it up! This is a great make-ahead meal, and extremely packable for lunches.

PRODUCE
2 cloves garlic
1-inch (2.5 cm) piece fresh ginger
2 limes
Handful fresh cilantro
¼ head red cabbage
2 watermelon radishes or 4 regular radishes
1 English cucumber
4 medium carrots
2 avocados, sliced
Handful fresh mint

PANTRY
1 tablespoon toasted sesame oil
1 tablespoon sriracha
¼ cup (60 ml) nut butter, store-bought or homemade (page 266), preferably peanut or cashew
12 ounces (340 g) dried rice noodles
Handful roasted, salted peanuts or cashews

Make the spicy peanut sauce: Grate 2 cloves garlic directly into a little bowl. Peel a 1-inch (2.5 cm) piece of fresh ginger and grate into the bowl using a Microplane. Add the juice of 1 lime, 1 tablespoon toasted sesame oil, 1 tablespoon sriracha, and ¼ cup (60 ml) nut butter and stir to combine. Add a tablespoon or two water to thin the sauce to your desired consistency. Finely chop a handful of cilantro and stir it in.

Prep the produce: Use a mandoline to (carefully) shave ¼ head red cabbage and 2 watermelon radishes. I like to pop the radishes in a bit of ice water while I continue working to crisp them up! Cut the cucumber into thin half-moons and use a julienne peeler on the 4 carrots. Slice the remaining lime into wedges.

Cook the noodles: Bring a medium pot of water to a boil. Add 12 ounces (340 g) noodles, cook according to the package instructions, drain, and rinse well with cool water. Put the noodles in a medium bowl and toss with the sauce to coat.

Assemble and serve: Divide the peanut noodles among four bowls, then group together little bunches of each of the veggies and sliced avocado on top of the noodles followed by a handful of fresh cilantro and mint leaves. Sprinkle with some crushed peanuts (or cashews) and serve with lime wedges.

SNACKS, STARTERS, SIDES & SALADS

Something I learned about myself while writing this book is that I cannot survive on snacks. I need full meals. I don't take a lot of little bites of things throughout the day. The moment to have snacks ready is when you're having people over; snacks will buy you some time. A gorgeous platter of colorful dips and crudités will take the attention off whatever else is still happening in the kitchen.

Starters, and sides, well, they are important too. Sometimes these are the little bites and flavors that make a meal the most memorable.

And salads, it turns out, are still what I love the most. I am inspired by the limitless possibilities of what a salad can be.

Charred Cabbage with Mushroom Butter

Serves 4 to 6 as a side

Charring vegetables is a magic trick. It pulls all the sweetness to the top and adds the richest, deepest smoky flavor, transforming the humble cabbage into something so special. Mushroom powder brings this cabbage into another dimension—swirled with a little butter, it becomes a tender, melt-in-your-mouth savory side, or, with a little rice and a crispy egg, it's satisfying enough to enjoy as a main course.

....

PRODUCE
1 medium green cabbage (about 2 pounds/900 g)

DAIRY
6 tablespoons (85 g) unsalted butter, plus more if needed

PANTRY
1 tablespoon neutral oil, such as sunflower or avocado
1 tablespoon mushroom powder
Brown rice vinegar
Flaky salt

Prep the cabbage: Remove the outer leaves of 1 green cabbage and cut it into quarters.

Cook the cabbage: Heat a cast-iron skillet over medium-high heat. Add 1 tablespoon neutral oil and the 4 wedges of cabbage. Cook the cabbage undisturbed until very dark on one side, darker than you think is normal or right, about 10 minutes.

Assemble the cabbage: Next, you will be doing a very cheffy thing here, called butter basting. Turn the heat down to medium-low and add the butter to the pan with the cabbage. Once it starts getting a little foamy, tilt the pan toward you a bit, and use a spoon to baste the butter over each cabbage wedge at its thickest part. Do this for about 30 seconds to a minute, then take a little break, and do it again a few more times. If the butter starts to get too dark, add another little knob. It's a little bit hard to test the cabbage for doneness with certainty, but a skewer should be able to be inserted deep into the cabbage fairly easily. Add 1 tablespoon mushroom powder to the butter, swirl it all around, and baste the cabbage wedges one more time.

Serve the cabbage: Carefully remove the cabbage from the pan, cut it into smaller pieces if desired, and drench with any butter left in the pan. Shake a little vinegar over the top and sprinkle with flaky salt.

Green Toddess Potato Salad

Serves 8 to 10 as a side

My friend Todd said this had to be in the book, so it is. A last-minute addition but completely addictive, and a crowd favorite. Not your boring old potato salad, but so simple!

PRODUCE
3 pounds (1.4 kg) small Yukon gold potatoes
1 bunch parsley
2 lemons
1 bunch green onions

DAIRY
½ cup (120 ml) buttermilk

PANTRY
Kosher salt and freshly ground black pepper
¼ cup (60 ml) mayonnaise

Cook the potatoes: Place 3 pounds (1.4 kg) small Yukon gold potatoes and 1 tablespoon salt in a large pot and cover with water by at least 2 inches (5 cm). Bring to a boil, reduce the heat slightly, and simmer until the potatoes are tender, about 12 to 14 minutes. Drain the potatoes well and place them back in the pot or in a serving bowl.

Make the green goddess dressing: In a food processor, combine 1 bunch parsley, ½ cup (120 ml) buttermilk, ¼ cup (60 ml) mayonnaise, the zest from 2 lemons, and the juice from 1 lemon. Season with salt and pepper.

Assemble and serve: Thinly slice the green onions and add them to the bowl with the potatoes. Add the dressing and toss everything together. Taste for seasoning and serve immediately.

Curried Carrot Dip

Makes 1 pint (480 ml)

It is hard to believe, but sometimes I get a little bit sick of hummus. This is a great dip to get some new flavor into the mix. Don't be afraid of the habanero; its heat is intense, but also wonderfully bright and fruity. Do wear gloves when handling them if you have them. Do remove the seeds. And don't touch anything . . . before washing your hands really, really well.

....

PRODUCE
6 carrots (about 1½ pounds/600 g total)
¼ to ½ habanero chile
Lime wedges
Cilantro leaves
Crudités, for serving

PANTRY
2 tablespoons coconut oil
Kosher salt
1 teaspoon cumin seeds
1 teaspoon mustard seeds
1 teaspoon coriander seeds
1 teaspoon ground turmeric
1 (15-ounce/430 g) can coconut cream
1 (14-ounce/400 g) can white beans
Seed Crackers (page 270)

Prep the carrots: Preheat the oven to 450ºF (230ºC). Peel 6 carrots and cut them into 2-inch (2.5 cm) long chunks.

Roast the carrots: Add the carrot chunks to a rimmed baking sheet along with 2 tablespoons coconut oil and a generous sprinkle of salt. Roast until the carrots are tender and charred in places, about 30 minutes. Stir the carrots on the sheet pan and add 1 teaspoon each of cumin seeds, mustard seeds, coriander seeds, and turmeric and toss to coat. Cook 5 more minutes, until the spices are toasted and fragrant.

Prep and add the chile: You'll want to deal with the habanero carefully. Wearing gloves if you have them, slice the chile open and scrape out the seeds. I suggest adding just one-quarter of the pepper to start. Make sure you wash your hands really well after handling.

Blend the dip: Put the roasted carrots into a food processor, scraping anything stuck on the pan too. Add one-quarter of the habanero and one 15-ounce (430 g) can coconut cream and one 14-ounce (400 g) can white beans and blend until well combined. Taste and if you want more heat, add another quarter of the habanero, and blend well. Taste again for seasoning and add more salt if desired. Serve with lime wedges, fresh cilantro leaves, crudités, and seed crackers.

Clockwise from top: Curried Carrot Dip (opposite), Beet Hummus with Lemony Labneh Swirl (page 142), and Fennel Tzatziki (page 143)

Beet Hummus with Lemony Labneh Swirl

Makes 1 quart (960 ml)

Two dips are better than one. This vibrant pink hummus gets a tangy, bright lift from the swirl of labneh with preserved lemon. Serve with crudités, pita, or the Seed Crackers on page 270. Make it vegan by using thick vegan yogurt instead of labneh.

....

PRODUCE
2 medium beets (about 4 ounces/120 g)
1 head garlic
2 lemons

DAIRY
¼ cup (60 ml) labneh or thick vegan yogurt

PANTRY
1 cup (200 g) dried chickpeas
Kosher salt and freshly ground black pepper
Extra-virgin olive oil
1 teaspoon baking soda
1 cup (240 ml) tahini
6 tablespoons (90 ml) ice water
½ preserved lemon

Prep the chickpeas: Soak 1 cup (200 g) chickpeas in cold water to cover for at least 8 hours, up to overnight.

Roast the beets and garlic: Preheat the oven to 425°F (220°C). Wash 2 beets and line a piece of foil with parchment paper. Place the beets in the center, sprinkle with plenty of salt and pepper, and drizzle with oil. Bring the two opposite ends of the foil to meet. Fold the edges over about 1 inch (2.5 cm) and then fold again to create a tight little packet. Cut the top third off 1 head of garlic, and repeat this process to make it its own little packet. Roast until the garlic is golden brown and tender, about 45 minutes. Roast the beets until they are tender when pierced with a knife, about 60 minutes.

Make the chickpeas: Drain the chickpeas and add them to a medium pot. Sprinkle with 1 teaspoon baking soda and cook over high heat, stirring constantly. Add enough water to cover the chickpeas by about 1 inch (2.5 cm). Bring to a simmer over medium-high heat and skim the surface as little bits of skin and foam float to the top. Lower the heat, cover, and cook until the chickpeas are very soft. Begin checking for doneness after 20 minutes, but it may take up to an hour, depending on how fresh your beans are.

Drain the chickpeas (you should have about 3 cups) and transfer to a food processor. Process until the chickpeas form a smooth, thick paste, and then add the roasted beets. Pulse to incorporate. Add 1 cup (240 ml) tahini, the juice of 2 lemons, garlic cloves, and 1 teaspoon salt. Drizzle in 6 tablespoons (90 ml) ice water and continue to process for another 5 minutes or so, until the hummus is smooth, silky, and dreamy.

Transfer to a bowl, cover with plastic wrap, and let rest about 30 minutes before serving, or refrigerate for up to 5 days. Let come to room temperature before serving.

Prepare the preserved-lemon labneh and serve: Just before you're ready to serve the hummus, remove the flesh from ½ of a preserved lemon so that just the ring of the peel remains. Add the lemon peel and ¼ cup (60 ml) labneh to a clean food processor and pulse to combine. Season with salt to taste. Use a spoon to swirl the labneh on top of the beet hummus, drizzle with olive oil, and serve.

Fennel Tzatziki

Makes 1 quart (945 ml)

Kismet, one of my favorite restaurants in LA, adds fennel to their tzatziki for some very welcome additional flavor. The inspiration for this recipe is a combination of that and my friend Angelo's mom's recipe. It's ultra-creamy, cooling, and truly delicious as a dip for veggies or pita, or on the cauliflower flatbreads on page 224.

··

PRODUCE
1 English cucumber
1 head fennel
½ cup (15 g) chopped fresh dill
4 cloves garlic
2 lemons

DAIRY
2 cups (480 ml) unsweetened plain or coconut
  yogurt
1 cup (240 ml) sour cream

PANTRY
Kosher salt

Prep the veggies: Peel 1 cucumber and grate it on the large holes of a box grater. Trim the fronds from a head of fennel and reserve (they store best when wrapped in a damp paper towel and put in a plastic bag). Grate the fennel bulb. Transfer the cucumber and fennel to a colander set over a bowl, sprinkle with 1 teaspoon salt, and let sit for 4 hours or up to overnight.

Make the dip and serve: Squeeze out all the additional liquid from the cucumber and fennel with your hands. Chop the fennel. Dump out any liquid in the bowl and wipe it dry. Using that bowl, mix together the cucumber mixture, 2 cups (480 ml) yogurt, 1 cup (240 ml) sour cream, ¼ cup (5 g) chopped fennel fronds, and ½ cup (15 g) chopped fresh dill. Use a Microplane to grate 4 cloves garlic right into the tzatziki, and then grate in the zest of 2 lemons. Add ¼ cup (60 ml) lemon juice. Mix well and taste for seasoning. It will keep for about 5 days in the fridge but will need a little mixing.

Nutritional Yeast Popcorn

Makes about 12 cups (140 g)

Even if you've never tried nutritional yeast before, I guarantee that after you taste this popcorn you'll be sneaking a jar of it into the movie theater.

....

PANTRY
2 tablespoons neutral oil, such as sunflower or avocado
½ cup (110 g) popcorn kernels
¼ cup (60 ml) extra-virgin olive oil
¼ cup (60 ml) nutritional yeast, plus more if needed
½ teaspoon kosher salt

Pop the corn: Add 2 tablespoons neutral oil to a large pot with a lid. Heat over medium-high. Once the oil is shimmering, add a few of the popcorn kernels, cover, and listen until they begin to pop—once they do, add the rest of the ½ cup (110 g) kernels. Cover, and then make sure that the oil is hot enough that the popcorn is popping, but not so hot that it's smoking—this is usually medium-low for me, but you'll have to do some adjusting and occasionally give the pot a good shake. The whole experience should take about 10 minutes.

Sprinkle and toss: Drizzle the popcorn with ¼ cup (60 ml) olive oil and add the ¼ cup (60 ml) nutritional yeast and a good pinch of salt. Shake to distribute the nutritional yeast and get it to stick to the popcorn, taste, and I guarantee you you'll want to add more.

Benny's Green Salsa

Makes about 4 cups (945 ml)

Benny Blanco is one of my best friends, even after we wrote an entire cookbook together.
I'm an only child and prefer to work alone, so it's a miracle that we collaborated, and I still
love him, even after he waited until the absolute last second to contribute a recipe to my book.
Benny is a sauce guy; he's always got something sticky or spicy to drizzle on top
of everything. This is his easiest salsa, and the one I always like to keep on hand for burritos
or eggs, or just eating with chips.

....

PRODUCE
6 tomatillos (20 ounces/555 g)
1 avocado
½ white onion
1 serrano pepper
1 lime

PANTRY
Salt
Tortilla chips, for serving

Prep the vegetables: Remove the husks from
6 tomatillos, peel and quarter the avocado, and quarter
the ½ white onion. Remove the stem from 1 serrano
pepper and cut in half. Juice the lime.

Blend the salsa: Add all the ingredients to a blender
with ¼ cup (60 ml) water and blend until smooth.
Season with a generous pinch of salt. Serve with tortilla
chips. Store in an airtight container in the fridge for
a week.

Zucchini and Corn Fritters

Makes 15

I love making little fritters like this in the summer—it's a quick way to use up the zucchini that is in season and absolutely everywhere. Instead of the all-purpose flour, you can use chickpea flour to add a little protein and make them gluten free! These may be fried, but they are packed with vegetables and incredibly satisfying. I think they are actually enough for a light meal, alongside a salad.

PRODUCE
2 large zucchini (about 14 ounces/400 g)
4 ears corn (about 2 cups corn)
4 green onions, both white and green parts finely chopped
1 lemon

DAIRY
Spiced Yogurt Sauce (page 276)

PROTEIN
4 large eggs, beaten

PANTRY
Kosher salt and freshly ground black pepper
¾ teaspoon kosher salt, plus more
1 cup (125 g) all-purpose flour, plus 2 tablespoons (15 g), if needed
Neutral oil, such as sunflower or avocado, for frying

Prep the fritter batter: Use a food processor with a grater attachment or the large holes of a box grater to grate 2 large zucchini. Transfer to a colander set over a large bowl or in the sink. Toss together with about 2 teaspoons salt and let sit for 15 to 20 minutes (or longer!) while you prepare the rest of the ingredients.

Quickly and with confidence, holding 1 ear of corn straight up and down on its base by the pointy tip, run a sharp knife repeatedly down the length of the cob to remove the kernels from the corn. Repeat with the 3 remaining ears of corn. There are a lot of tricks on the internet for doing this without making a mess, but I think it's really better and safer to just work swiftly but carefully. Transfer to a large bowl.

Using your hands, squeeze out as much of the water as possible from the zucchini. I sometimes also like to put the zucchini in a clean kitchen towel and wring out as much liquid as I can that way. Transfer to the bowl with the corn. Stir in 4 finely chopped green onions (white and green parts), 4 large beaten eggs, and 1 cup (125 g) flour. Season with a bit of salt and pepper.

Cook the fritters and serve: Add ¼ inch (5 mm) neutral oil to a large cast-iron skillet and heat over medium-high. Add a corn kernel to the oil and once it bubbles and sizzles you will know the oil is ready.

Working in batches, use a 2-ounce (60 g) scoop to add batter to the pan. You should be able to fit 3 or 4 fritters per batch. Squish the fritters down a bit with a fish spatula. Cook until golden brown, 2 to 3 minutes, and then flip carefully and cook until golden brown on the other side, about 2 minutes more.

Transfer the fritters to a little stack of paper towels (or some paper bags) to soak up excess oil. Serve the hot fritters with the yogurt sauce and a sprinkle of flaky salt.

Little Gems with Nutritional Yeast Tahini Dressing, Sunflower Seeds, and Avocado

Serves 4 as a side

This dressing is the best, and I want to eat it on everything and use it as a dip.
I love this combination of smooth avocado, crisp-crunchy little gem lettuce, and toasty roasted
sunflower seeds. Add your favorite protein for a complete meal.

PRODUCE
1 lemon
4 heads little gem lettuce
2 avocados

PANTRY
2 tablespoons nutritional yeast
2 tablespoons tahini
1 tablespoon apple cider vinegar
1 teaspoon honey
Extra-virgin olive oil
Kosher salt
¼ cup (35 g) roasted salted sunflower seeds

Make the nutritional yeast tahini dressing: In a small bowl, whisk together 2 tablespoons nutritional yeast, 2 tablespoons tahini, 1 tablespoon apple cider vinegar, juice of 1 lemon, 1 teaspoon honey, and ¼ cup (60 ml) extra-virgin olive oil. Add water 1 tablespoon at a time until it reaches your desired consistency. Season with salt.

Prep the produce: Clean and dry 4 little gems, separating the leaves. Peel and slice the avocados.

Assemble and serve: In a bowl or platter arrange the clean lettuce leaves. Drizzle with dressing or toss with the leaves. Top with avocado slices and sunflower seeds and serve immediately.

Bass Crudo with Chile, Radish, and Nasturtiums

Serves 4 to 6 as a starter

Every summer, the only thing I want to eat is crudo. When it's hot and sticky, sometimes a whole meal is just too much. The freshest fish thinly sliced and ice cold, with spicy shaved veggies, sweet, juicy cherry tomatoes, and a generous pool of olive oil—I had this one . . . a lot. I love it with a buttered piece of warm focaccia and a salad. It's an elegant meal that comes together quickly on nights when it's too hot to cook.

PRODUCE
½ pint (145 g) sungolds or other sweet cherry tomatoes
1 Fresno chile
1 small shallot
2 radishes
Handful nasturtium blossoms and small nasturtium leaves (optional)

PROTEIN
8 ounces (225 g) sushi-grade skinless bass fillet

PANTRY
Extra-virgin olive oil
Flaky salt

Prep: Using tweezers, remove any pin bones from 8 ounces (225 g) skinless bass fillet. Place the bass on a serving plate in the freezer while you prep the vegetables.

Cut ½ pint (145 g) sweet cherry tomatoes in half. Using a mandoline or sharp knife, thinly slice ½ to 1 whole Fresno chile, depending on how spicy you like it, 1 shallot, and 2 radishes.

Once the fish is just a little frozen—enough that it's a bit firmer, 10 to 15 minutes—use a very sharp knife to thinly slice it. The crudo doesn't need to be razor thin, anywhere between the thickness of a coin or ¼ inch (6 mm) will do, depending on your preference.

Assemble and serve: Arrange the sliced fish on the chilled serving platter. Scatter the tomatoes, shallots, and radishes over the top. Drizzle with olive oil, sprinkle with flaky salt, and top with a handful of nasturtium blossoms and petals and small leaves, if using. Serve right away.

Asparagus Cooked in Its Own Juice

Serves 4 to 6 as a side

One particularly beautiful summer evening, Ben and I put on nice outfits and walked across the Manhattan Bridge in impractical shoes, and he led me to a little place in Chinatown called GEM. I'm not always won over by fancy little bites of food on a tasting menu, but a simple plate of asparagus cooked in asparagus juice really got me. It somehow makes it taste . . . greener . . . fresher . . . This side makes any simple meal of chicken or fish feel instantly more elegant.

PRODUCE
2 large bunches asparagus

DAIRY
1 tablespoon unsalted butter

PANTRY
Kosher salt and freshly ground black pepper

Prep the asparagus: Trim the woody ends from 2 large bunches asparagus, and use a Y-peeler to peel the lower parts of the stems. Add the woody ends to a blender with 3 cups (710 ml) water and puree until smooth.

Cook and serve: Strain through a fine-mesh sieve and add the asparagus juice to a straight-sided skillet. Season well with salt and pepper. Add the asparagus to the pan. Bring to a simmer and cook until just tender, 3 to 4 minutes, and serve immediately.

Furikake Glazed Squash

Serves 4 to 6 as a side

Furikake, a Japanese condiment made with sesame, nori, and dried fish, is a magical ingredient, and I love the way its salty, funky flavor pairs with the natural sweetness of squash. A little bit of honey helps the squash caramelize and get roasty-toasty. You could serve this over rice with some greens or a piece of baked or broiled fish for a full meal.

....

PRODUCE
2 delicata or acorn squash

PANTRY
¼ cup (60 ml) honey
2 tablespoons soy sauce
2 tablespoons neutral oil, such as sunflower or avocado
2 tablespoons furikake

Prep the squash: Preheat the oven to 400°F (205°C). Line a baking sheet with parchment paper.

If using a delicata squash, slice into ½-inch (12 mm) rounds. If using an acorn squash, cut in half, remove the seeds, and slice into slightly thicker crescents.

In a large bowl, whisk together ¼ cup (60 ml) honey, 2 tablespoons soy sauce, and a good drizzle of neutral oil. Add the sliced squash to the bowl and toss to coat.

Roast the squash: Arrange the squash in a single layer on the prepared baking sheet. Roast until the squash is tender, flipping once, halfway through, 20 to 25 minutes. Sprinkle with 2 tablespoons furikake and serve.

Creamy Sesame Carrot Salad

Serves 4 to 6 as a side

Benny and our friend Simon had the brilliant idea to use a traditional Japanese goma (sesame) dressing on carrots instead of on the usual gomae (spinach salad) we love to make. Sesame and carrot are a combination made in heaven. They balance each other perfectly, and I love the crunch of eating the carrots raw.

PRODUCE
6 large carrots (about 1 pound/454 g)

PANTRY
¼ cup plus 2 tablespoons (45 g) toasted sesame seeds
2 tablespoons soy sauce
1 tablespoon mirin
1 teaspoon honey
1 tablespoon sake (optional)

Prep the sesame seeds: Using a mortar and pestle or spice grinder, grind ¼ cup (30 g) toasted sesame seeds until they are almost completely smooth and transfer them to a large bowl. Grind the remaining 2 tablespoons sesame seeds just a little bit—this will add some nice texture to the salad. Add to the bowl.

Assemble and serve: Whisk in 2 tablespoons soy sauce, 1 tablespoon mirin, and 1 teaspoon honey (and if you have sake on hand, a splash of dry sake is delicious here!). Use a julienne peeler to shave 6 large carrots or the grating attachment on your food processor. You can also cut or grate by hand! Toss everything together and taste for seasoning. Serve immediately. You can eat the leftovers—they will stand up to the fridge overnight—but it's really best enjoyed right away.

Big Green Gingery Salad

Serves 4 as a starter

What do I want to eat after developing an entire book of inventive salads? Just a simple green salad, using the freshest lettuces I can find. Something crisp, piled high, that goes with absolutely anything. Besides finding great lettuces, the only key is to wash all the lettuces gently in a salad spinner and dry them well. Add a piece of protein and this is a simple, satisfying meal.

PRODUCE
2-inch (5 cm) piece fresh ginger
1 tablespoon fresh lime juice
2 avocados
1 head butter lettuce, leaves separated

PANTRY
¼ cup (60 ml) rice vinegar
1½ teaspoons honey
6 tablespoons (90 ml) neutral oil, such as
  sunflower or avocado
Kosher salt
Gomasio (see page 28), for serving

Make the ginger vinaigrette: Peel a 2-inch (5 cm) piece fresh ginger and use a Microplane to grate it into a small bowl. Add ¼ cup (60 ml) rice vinegar, 1 tablespoon fresh lime juice, 1½ teaspoons honey, and 6 tablespoons (90 ml) neutral oil and stir gently to combine. Season with salt to taste.

Assemble and serve: Peel, pit, and slice 2 avocados. Gently pile the lettuce leaves on a plate, drizzling with a bit of vinaigrette as you build and making sure to get in all of the lettuce's nooks and crannies. Nestle pieces of sliced avocado into the leaves. Once you're done building, drizzle with more dressing, sprinkle with gomasio, and serve.

HEALTH FOOD FROM THE SOURCE

A book about health food could not be complete without a recipe from Jim Baker's (aka Father Yod's) LA health food restaurant, the Source (see the next page for the Aware Salad). I never had the chance to go to the restaurant while it was open, but I've loved living vicariously through friends who remember going there throughout the seventies and eighties to see celebrities and beautiful waitresses and eat Magic Mushrooms and Mashed Yeast. I did, however, get to meet some of the Source Family during the last week of writing this book, while sitting at a long table drenched in sunshine in the mountains of Malibu, which was both divine timing and an incredible experience.

Isis Aquarian helped paint a clearer picture of what walking through the doors of the Source restaurant was like, and I loved the way she explained it:

"As soon as you stepped onto the patio, people didn't know what hit them. They just wanted to be there. Why was the food so good? What the hell? It was just a frequency, a higher frequency. Businessmen would come in suits and started feeling peaceful. Everyone knew they wouldn't be bothered . . . Celebrities would come in and no one would come over and take photos . . . They felt safe."

Isis also told me there was a sign in the kitchen that Father Yod hung that said "Maintain the Standard," and this was key. "Once a recipe was set, we maintained it — the food was made with that same intention time and time again . . . If someone was having an off day, was negative, crying, or hurt, or they didn't have [the] right vibration, they were asked to leave for the day . . . and [were] not allowed to work, because whatever vibration the food is being made with, you're going to be eating it."

The Source Aware Salad

Serves 2 as a meal, 4 as a starter or side

Since Isis Aquarian gave me this recipe, it has become an almost daily staple in our house. Ben and I take turns making it, and sometimes we will shred a big batch of veggies so it's easier to assemble for a couple of days. It seems like eating it every day could be one of the answers to life. Don't forget to Maintain the Standard.

···

PRODUCE
1 lemon
3 tablespoons finely chopped fresh dill
3 tablespoons finely chopped fresh chives
1 head romaine or 3 heads little gem lettuce
½ head red cabbage
3 stalks celery
1 pint (290 g) cherry tomatoes
1 avocado
½ English cucumber
4 medium carrots
2 medium beets
1 cup (90 g) broccoli or alfalfa sprouts

PANTRY
1 tablespoon whole-grain mustard
2 tablespoons white wine vinegar
¼ teaspoon onion powder
¼ teaspoon garlic powder
¼ cup (60 ml) olive oil
Kosher salt and freshly ground black pepper
¼ cup (35 g) roasted sunflower seeds
¼ cup (35 g) pine nuts, toasted (see page 33)

Make the source family dressing: In a bowl, combine the juice of 1 lemon, 3 tablespoons fresh dill, 3 tablespoons fresh chives, 1 tablespoon whole-grain mustard, 2 tablespoons white wine vinegar, ¼ teaspoon onion powder, ¼ teaspoon garlic powder, ¼ cup (60 ml) olive oil, and salt and pepper to taste, and whisk to combine, or add to a jar with a tight-fitting lid and shake. Make sure to taste for seasoning. Store any leftover dressing in an airtight container in the fridge for up to 1 week.

Prep the salad: While you could just make one big salad, I like to make individual servings and build each bowl up as I go. Start with chopping 1 head romaine to create the base, and put half in each of your two serving bowls. Then use a mandoline or box grater to very thinly shave half a head of red cabbage and bunch it together in a small pile on top of the romaine in each bowl. Since I have my mandoline out, I use it to thinly slice 3 stalks celery, then I add that evenly around the bowls. Next halve 1 pint (290 g) cherry tomatoes and group the halves together on top of each salad. Slice 1 avocado and fan the slices on one side of each bowl. Slice half an English cucumber into half-moons and gather those together on top of the lettuce in each salad. Peel 4 carrots and grate on the large holes of a box grater, and keep building by adding a pile of carrots to each salad. Always save the beets for last unless you want everything to be pink. (Wear gloves if you don't want pink hands.) Peel 2 beets and grate with the box grater and arrange in small piles next to the carrots.

Assemble and serve: Place half of the sprouts in the center of each bowl. Drizzle with a generous amount of the dressing and sprinkle with ¼ cup (35 g) sunflower seeds and ¼ cup (35 g) pine nuts, dividing them evenly between the salad bowls.

Silken Tofu Salad for Lauryn

Serves 2 as a meal

My friend Lauryn grew up in LA, so I love to hear her wax poetic about the health food she grew up eating. This is a salad she has been dreaming about for a long time, and there really is something perfect about it. Two dressings! You might think it's a lot of work, but it's really not that bad, plus the tahini dressing is particularly delicious to have on hand and use as a dip for veggies throughout the week.

PRODUCE
2-inch (5 cm) piece fresh ginger
2 large carrots (140 g)
½ English cucumber
½ small daikon radish
4 ounces (115 g) sugar snap peas
4 ounces (115 g) white button mushrooms
1 avocado
½ cup (20 g) radish sprouts

PROTEIN
½ block (8 ounces/227 g) silken tofu

PANTRY
¼ cup (60 ml) tahini
¼ cup (60 ml) Kewpie mayonnaise
2 tablespoons rice vinegar
2 teaspoons soy sauce
4 teaspoons honey
1 tablespoon plus 2 teaspoons toasted sesame oil
1 tablespoon ponzu (the citrusy, salty Japanese condiment)
2 tablespoons neutral oil, such as sunflower or avocado
Gomasio (see page 28), for serving

Make the tahini ginger dressing: In a small bowl, peel and grate a 2-inch (5 cm) piece fresh ginger. Add ¼ cup (60 ml) tahini, ¼ cup (60 ml) mayonnaise, 1 tablespoon of the rice vinegar, 2 teaspoons soy sauce, 2 teaspoons of the honey, and 2 teaspoons of the toasted sesame oil and whisk to combine. Thin with 2 to 3 tablespoons of water, adding 1 tablespoon at a time.

Make the ponzu vinaigrette: In another small bowl, whisk together 1 tablespoon ponzu, the remaining 1 tablespoon rice vinegar, 2 tablespoons neutral oil, and remaining 1 tablespoon toasted sesame oil.

Prep the salad ingredients: Cut 8 ounces (227 g) silken tofu into 1-inch (2.5 cm) cubes. Use a julienne peeler to cut 2 large carrots into matchsticks. Julienne half an English cucumber, half a small daikon, and 4 ounces (115 g) sugar snap peas. Thinly slice 4 ounces (115 g) white mushrooms and 1 avocado.

Assemble and serve: Add a little of the ponzu vinaigrette to the bottom of a serving platter, then arrange the tofu, carrots, cucumbers, daikon, peas, mushrooms, and sprouts on the platter, grouping the ingredients in small bunches and fanning out the avocado slices, as shown in the photo. Drizzle with the tahini dressing, sprinkle with the gomasio, and serve. Store any leftover tahini dressing in an airtight container for up to 1 week.

Heirloom Tomatoes and Chili Crisp

Serves 6 to 8 as a side

When tomatoes are at their peak, pick a variety of colors and shapes and sizes for this salad and bring in some cherry tomatoes too. Be generous with the chili crisp, and take the time to make your own. It is really simple, and you'll love having a big batch of it on hand at all times. I don't think this salad needs anything else, but I do sometimes garnish with some marigold or nasturtium petals if I have them on hand, or a few sprigs of cilantro. And it wouldn't be a bad idea to serve some salty feta cheese or crusty bread along with it.

....

PRODUCE
3 small shallots
2 heads garlic, cloves separated (you should have about 20 cloves)
3-inch (7.5 cm) piece fresh ginger
2 pounds (910 g) assorted heirloom and cherry tomatoes

PANTRY
1½ cups (360 ml) safflower or peanut oil
¼ cup (25 g) crushed red pepper flakes
1 tablespoon honey
2 tablespoons soy sauce
¼ teaspoon ground cinnamon
Flaky salt

Make the chili crisp: Peel and thinly slice 3 shallots and the cloves from 2 heads garlic on a mandoline or with a sharp knife. They should be thinner than a coin. Add the shallots and garlic to a small pot with 1½ cups (360 ml) safflower oil. Simmer over medium heat for 15 to 20 minutes. You want the shallots and garlic cloves to be deep golden brown, but not too brown (or they will become bitter!).

Meanwhile, peel a 3-inch (7.5 cm) piece fresh ginger. Using a Microplane, grate the ginger into a small heatproof bowl (you should have about 2 tablespoons), then add ¼ cup (25 g) red pepper flakes, 1 tablespoon honey, 2 tablespoons soy sauce, and ¼ teaspoon cinnamon.

Carefully strain the pot of garlic and shallots through a fine-mesh sieve over the heatproof bowl. Let the crispy bits continue to crisp up on a paper towel–lined plate, and let your oil sit until it cools to room temperature, then stir the crisp bits into the seasoned oil.

Assemble and serve: Slice the tomatoes and arrange them on a platter. Drizzle with a generous amount of chili crisp. Add a little flaky salt and serve. Transfer the extra chili crisp to an airtight container and store in the fridge for up to 1 month.

Chopped Cucumber and Feta Salad

Serves 4 as a side

The salad that goes with everything. Make this to go alongside your favorite protein, sandwich, burger, pasta, or truly anything. Throw in leftovers, canned tuna, or some crispy chickpeas. Everything just gets chopped and tossed together—crunchy, herbaceous, fresh, salty, and bright.

....

PRODUCE
4 Persian cucumbers
3 heads little gem lettuce or 1 romaine heart
1 cup (250 g) green olives, such as Cerignola
4 green onions
Big handful fresh dill
Big handful fresh mint leaves
Big handful fresh parsley leaves
1 lemon

DAIRY
½ cup (75 g) feta cheese

PANTRY
Extra-virgin olive oil
Kosher salt and freshly ground black pepper

Prep the veggies: Finely dice 4 Persian cucumbers and add them to a big bowl. Chop 3 heads little gem lettuce and add to the bowl. Remove the pits from 1 cup (250 g) green olives and chop them, then add to the bowl. Thinly slice the white and green parts of 4 green onions, chop the big handfuls of dill, mint, and parsley, and add them all to the bowl.

Assemble and serve: Crumble ½ cup (75 g) feta into the salad bowl. Give everything a good toss. Add the juice of 1 lemon and a heavy glug of olive oil with a pinch of salt and pepper. Toss everything again and taste for seasoning.

Raw Snap Peas with Feta, Chile, and Mint

Serves 4 to 6 as a side

I have always loved raw peas. When they are in season and exceptionally sweet, it's hard to beat the fresh flavor of a snap pea, which to me is really the taste of spring itself. One beautiful day my friend Pierce Abernathy came over and whipped up this simple salad. The peas are perfectly crunchy, the lemon juice and zest add so much brightness, and the salty tang of the feta cheese rounds it out to have the perfect balance of flavors.

PRODUCE
1 pound (454 g) sugar snap peas
1 lemon
Handful fresh mint leaves

DAIRY
6 ounces (170 g) soft feta cheese

PANTRY
Extra-virgin olive oil
Crushed red pepper flakes
Flaky salt

Prep the peas: Trim 1 pound (454 g) snap peas. Use a small sharp knife and hold each pea with its curve facing you. Trim the top and pull off the tough string that zips up the pea. Once all the peas are trimmed and unzipped, thinly slice them on a diagonal. Add to a large bowl.

Assemble and serve: Toss the peas with the zest and juice of 1 lemon, a generous amount of olive oil, and 6 ounces (170 g) crumbled soft feta cheese. Sprinkle with fresh mint leaves and some crushed red pepper flakes and flaky salt to serve.

Peach and Burrata Caprese with Hot Honey

Serves 4 to 6 as a side

My next book will be called *Everybody Loves Caprese* because it is just the truth. Everyone does, and there are a million ways to play around with it. I love this version because it is a little surprising. It is sweet and juicy but has a secret little kick and a super-mild nuttiness and crunch from the poppy seeds.

PRODUCE
6 ripe peaches
1 lime

DAIRY
8 ounces (225 g) burrata

PANTRY
2 tablespoons hot honey, such as Zab's, or
  2 tablespoons honey plus 1 teaspoon crushed
  red pepper flakes
Extra-virgin olive oil
1 teaspoon poppy seeds
Handful fresh basil leaves
Flaky salt

Prep the fruit and cheese: Pit and slice 6 ripe peaches and arrange the slices on a platter. Break up 8 ounces (225 g) burrata into manageable pieces everyone can grab and nestle them among the peaches.

Assemble and serve: Drizzle with 2 tablespoons hot honey and a little olive oil. Zest the lime and then squeeze the juice of half the lime over the peaches. Scatter 1 teaspoon poppy seeds and a handful of fresh basil leaves on top of everything and sprinkle with flaky salt.

Health Nut

Smashed Beets with Oranges, Rosey Harissa, and Whipped Goat Cheese

Serves 4 to 6 as a side

"If you can smash a potato, why can't you smash a beet?" I wondered. Well, you can, and it gets wonderfully craggy and crispy and soaks up all the delicious flavor of this smoky rosey harissa. This is one of those magical late-fall dishes that helps you enjoy early citrus, and you can make it all winter to brighten up your days. I really love it with tart blood oranges. Make it vegan by just using a cloud of coconut yogurt on the bottom.

PRODUCE
4 bunches small beets (about 30 ounces/855 g)
4 blood oranges

DAIRY
¾ cup (180 ml) unsweetened plain or coconut yogurt
5 ounces (140 g) goat cheese, room temperature

PANTRY
Kosher salt and freshly ground black pepper
Extra-virgin olive oil
Rosey Harissa (page 274)
Flaky salt

Cook the beets: Trim 4 bunches small beets and scrub them well. Add them to a large pot, cover with water by 2 inches (5 cm), and season generously with salt. Bring to a boil and cook the beets until tender when pierced with a knife, about 30 minutes. Remove the beets from the water and let cool until cool enough to handle.

Preheat the oven to 450°F (230°C). Using a paper towel, remove the skin from the beets. Place the beets on a rimmed baking sheet and smash by pressing down on them with a bowl or heavy skillet. Drizzle the baking

sheet with a good amount of oil and season with salt and a generous amount of pepper. Roast the smashed beets until crispy on both sides, 30 to 35 minutes, flipping once.

Prep the oranges: While the beets are roasting, prepare the 4 blood oranges. Using a sharp knife, cut the ends off each orange so it can stand up securely. Run the knife along the curve of the oranges, removing the peel and pith to expose the flesh. Once all the peel and pith are removed, slice the oranges.

Make the whipped goat cheese: In a food processor, combine the yogurt and the goat cheese. Season with salt and whip until smooth.

Assemble and serve: Spread the cheese on the bottom of a plate with a silicone spatula. Top with the roasted beets and orange slices. Spoon the rosey harissa over the top, and sprinkle with flaky salt.

Charred Broccoli Salad with Almonds and Spicy Green Goddess

Serves 4 as a side

Extremely charred broccoli makes for such a great salad. I dream of the burnt broccoli salad from Superiority Burger in the East Village. Brooks Headley, the chef, is really a vegetable wizard; he always comes up with the most brilliant combinations that are so unique, and just work so well. Nothing could be more perfect than that salad, but this plays with some of the sweet, spicy salty, charred flavors that I love so much about that dish.

PRODUCE
½ serrano pepper
1 lemon
4 green onions, trimmed
Handful fresh parsley
Handful fresh cilantro
1 clove garlic
2 heads broccoli (about 1 pound/454 g)
½ small red onion

DAIRY
⅓ cup (75 ml) unsweetened plain or coconut
   yogurt

PANTRY
¼ cup (60 ml) extra-virgin olive oil
2 anchovies
Kosher salt
5 pitted, dried Medjool dates
2 tablespoons rice vinegar
½ cup (46 g) sliced almonds, toasted (see
   page 33)
2 tablespoons hemp seeds

Make the spicy green goddess dressing: Combine ½ serrano pepper, the juice of ½ lemon, 4 green onions, 1 handful parsley and 1 handful cilantro, 1 clove garlic, ¼ cup (60 ml) extra-virgin olive oil, 2 anchovies, and ⅓ cup (75 ml) yogurt in a food processor. Blend until smooth, then season to taste with salt.

Make the salad: Cut the stems off 2 heads broccoli, peel and thinly slice them, and then cut the tops into florets. Heat a cast-iron skillet over high-ish heat and cook the broccoli until charred, 10 to 15 minutes.

Thinly slice ½ red onion and chop 5 dates.

Assemble and serve: In a large bowl, toss the charred broccoli florets and stems and onions with 2 tablespoons vinegar and season with salt. Finish with the dates, ½ cup (46 g) toasted almonds, and 2 tablespoons hemp seeds.

Lemony Kale Salad with Crispy Chickpeas and Avocado

Serves 2 as a meal, 4 as a side

Everyone needs a kale salad in their back pocket. This is a good, easy one to have down. Just make sure to massage your kale, please! This will hold up in the fridge really well for leftovers the next day, even after being dressed. It also is really delicious in a wrap for lunch with a layer of turkey and cheese for extra protein!

....

PRODUCE
1 lemon
½ small shallot
1 bunch curly kale (about 12 ounces/340 g)
1 avocado

DAIRY
Parmesan cheese

PANTRY
1 (14-ounce/400 g) can chickpeas
¼ cup (60 ml) extra-virgin olive oil, plus more for drizzling
½ teaspoon garlic powder
Kosher salt and freshly ground black pepper
1 teaspoon whole-grain mustard
1 teaspoon honey
¼ cup (46 g) pine nuts, toasted (see page 33)

Make the crispy chickpeas: Preheat the oven to 425°F (220°C). Drain one 14-ounce (400 g) can chickpeas, rinse, and transfer them to a rimmed baking sheet. Using a few paper towels or a clean kitchen towel, cover the chickpeas and roll the towels around a bit to absorb all the water. Toss with a few tablespoons of olive oil and ½ teaspoon garlic powder and season well with salt and pepper. Microplane a couple tablespoons Parmesan and the zest of 1 lemon (save the lemon for the vinaigrette) directly onto the chickpeas and give it all a good mix with your hands. Roast until very crispy and golden brown, about 20 minutes, tossing once.

Meanwhile, make the perfect lemony vinaigrette: Peel and mince ½ shallot and add to a small bowl or jar. Add the juice of 1 lemon, 1 teaspoon whole-grain mustard, ¼ cup (60 ml) olive oil, and 1 teaspoon honey. Shake vigorously or whisk and then season to taste with salt and pepper.

Assemble and serve: Add a few tablespoons of vinaigrette to a medium bowl (you can always add more, but you can't take it away if you've over-dressed). Strip the kale from its thick stems. Give it a good chop and add to the bowl. Massage the vinaigrette into the kale for a few minutes with your hands until the leaves begin to soften. Slice 1 avocado. Add the avocado slices and crispy chickpeas to the bowl and sprinkle with ¼ cup (46 g) pine nuts and a bit of Parmesan before serving.

Citrus with Dates, Olives, and Pistachios

Serves 4 to 6 as a side

I made this for my parents when they came out to visit me in California in January, peak citrus season. It's the best time to be here, really; I would even say it's magical. When there are so many oranges, you'll find ways to incorporate them into every meal. They don't need the sweetness of chopped dates, but the texture is really nice and a good balance to the brininess of the olives.

PRODUCE
4 blood oranges
3 Cara Cara oranges

PANTRY
½ cup (90 g) Cerignola olives
3 pitted, dried Medjool dates, chopped
¼ cup (30 g) pistachios, finely chopped
Best-quality extra-virgin olive oil
Flaky salt
Crushed red pepper flakes

Prep the oranges: Cut off both ends of 4 blood oranges so they can stand upright, then use a sharp knife to cut along the curve of each orange, removing its peel and pith to reveal the flesh. Cut the oranges into ¼-inch (6 mm) wheels. Arrange the slices on a platter.

Assemble and serve: Crush ½ cup (90 g) Cerignola olives with the flat side of a knife to remove the pits and scatter on top of the oranges along with 3 chopped dates and ¼ cup (30 g) finely chopped pistachios. Drizzle with some extra-virgin olive oil, sprinkle with flaky salt and red pepper flakes, and serve!

Planet Bliss Mesclun Salad with Fried Tofu Croutons

Serves 2 to 4 as a light meal or side

Sebastian Bliss was an amazing teacher to learn from, for a lot of reasons, but the biggest thing he showed me was how much love you can put in your food, night after night. This salad is the first salad I can remember being obsessed with, and craving. It was a constant on the menu, and I almost always ordered it for staff meal. I remember everyone ordering this salad: Simon Doonan and Jonathan Adler (and their sweet little Norfolk Terrier, Liberace) would order it with hummus on the side (which is a wonderful way to eat it and make it a meal). I wish you could have experienced eating this salad sitting under the porch on Shelter Island in the summer, but now you can have it anytime, anywhere. Thank you, Sebastian!

PRODUCE
¼ head red cabbage (about 12 ounces/160 g)
5 ounces (142 g) mesclun mix

PROTEIN
1 (14-ounce/397 g) block extra-firm tofu

PANTRY
1 teaspoon Dijon mustard
2 tablespoons balsamic vinegar
½ teaspoon honey
1 tablespoon mayonnaise
Kosher salt and freshly ground black pepper
2 tablespoons smoked soy sauce, or regular
 soy sauce and ½ teaspoon smoked paprika
2 tablespoons (15 g) cornstarch
Neutral oil, such as sunflower or avocado
1 cup (160 g) walnuts, toasted (see page 33)

Make the balsamic vinaigrette: In a large bowl, whisk together 1 teaspoon Dijon, 2 tablespoons balsamic vinegar, ½ teaspoon honey, and 1 tablespoon mayonnaise. Set aside (you'll mix the salad in later!).

Prep the tofu: Press 1 14-ounce (397 g) block tofu using a tofu press or cut the tofu lengthwise into 5 pieces and press using paper towels or clean dish towels and a heavy pan. Once some of the moisture has been released, cut into 1-inch (2.5 cm) pieces. Season with a bit of salt and 2 tablespoons smoked soy sauce (or regular soy and ½ teaspoon smoked paprika). Sprinkle with 2 tablespoons cornstarch.

Fry the tofu: Heat 3 cups (750 ml) neutral oil over medium-high in a wok or deep-sided skillet, to 350°F (175°C) if you have an instant-read thermometer. Add a piece of tofu, and once it is sizzling, carefully add the rest. Cook in two batches, until golden brown and crispy on all sides, 5 to 7 minutes. Let drain on a paper towel–lined plate.

Make the cabbage: Use a mandoline or a knife to very thinly shave ¼ head red cabbage. Heat a skillet over medium-high and add a bit of neutral oil. Sauté the cabbage until crisp-tender, about 5 minutes. Season with salt and pepper.

Assemble and serve: Add 5 ounces (140 g) mesclun mix, the cabbage, and walnuts to the bowl with the vinaigrette and toss. Top with the tofu and serve.

PLANT-FORWARD MAIN DISHES

I like to eat mostly vegetables. I have been a strict
vegetarian for long periods of time and today I am mostly
a vegetarian, but every once in a while, I eat a
(free-range organic) roasted chicken or a piece of fish.
I love vegetables, and these meals reflect that.

Many of these dishes can be made in under 45 minutes,
and I tried to make it so that there weren't weird bits of
things leftover, or a thousand dirty dishes, or too many trips
to the store or stores. I used Tokyo turnips again in a recipe,
but I swear I offer substitutions (I had an excess of them in
my garden this year!).

Eating healthy doesn't have to mean that it is harder to
make food that tastes good, and it certainly does not mean
that you can't be satisfied. These dishes are what I consider
to be comfort food; they're what I crave.

Zucchini and Pistachio Pesto Pizza

Serves 4

Ben's dad, Bill, adapted his favorite Smitten Kitchen pizza recipe so that it had less dairy in it for me—and his (genius) addition of pesto adds *so* much delicious flavor to this veggie-topped pizza. We make pizza all the time, and this is our go-to that quickly becomes everyone's favorite. If you're a gardener, it is an excellent way to use up a big zucchini bounty. Try it with a little chili crisp on top for some heat.

....

PRODUCE
3 large zucchini (about 2½ pounds/1.13 kg)
1 lemon

PANTRY
1 pound (454 g) pizza dough
Kosher salt and freshly ground black pepper
¼ cup (15 g) panko breadcrumbs
Extra-virgin olive oil
1 recipe Pistachio Pesto (page 274)
¼ cup Parmesan cheese, plus more for serving
Chili crisp, store-bought or homemade (page 169), or crushed red pepper flakes, for serving

Prep: Preheat the oven to 500°F (260°C) with a pizza stone in the top rack, if you have one. If you have a pizza oven, heat it to 900°F (500°C) if it can get that high! Bring the dough out of the refrigerator to relax at room temperature while you prep the zucchini.

Prep the veggies: Use a food processor with a grater attachment or the large holes of a box grater to grate 3 zucchini. Transfer to a colander set over a large bowl or in the sink. Toss together the zucchini and about ½ teaspoon salt and let sit for at least 30 minutes to release some of its water. Using your hands, squeeze out as much of the water as possible from the zucchini. I sometimes also like to put the zucchini in a clean

kitchen towel and wring out as much liquid as I can that way.

In a small bowl, toss together ¼ cup (15 g) bread-crumbs, a little drizzle of olive oil, and the zest of 1 lemon and season with salt.

Cook the pizza: If cooking the pizza in your home oven, brush a half sheet pan with a generous amount of oil. The dough should be relaxed now, and easier to stretch across the bottom of the pan. Use your fingers to push it to the edges as evenly as possible. Spread the pesto on the dough, leaving a small border around the edges, and then top with the zucchini. Sprinkle with the breadcrumb mixture and bake until the top is golden brown, 20 to 25 minutes.

Alternatively, if you have a pizza oven, assemble the pizza as described above, but stop after the zucchini. Bake until the crust begins to puff and the zucchini begins to brown, 2 to 3 minutes, then remove from the oven and carefully sprinkle with breadcrumbs. Return to the oven and bake until the breadcrumbs are golden, about 1 minute more.

Slice and serve: Wait for the pizza to cool for a minute before cutting into rectangles (or slices if it's a regular pie) and serve, sprinkled with chili crisp or red pepper flakes.

Skillet Spanakopita

Serves 8

Spanakopita has always been one of my favorite things to eat, but making it can be a bit tedious because of the chores of blanching the spinach and squeezing out all the liquid and folding up the phyllo into little individual triangles. Well, thank you again to Deb Perelman (Smitten Kitchen) for showing me that the spinach step is unnecessary! This dinner comes together fast, and there is enough for leftovers the next day.

PRODUCE
1 pound (454 g) baby spinach
½ yellow onion
½ cup (15 g) chopped fresh dill
½ cup (16 g) chopped fresh parsley
6 green onions
2 lemons

DAIRY
12 ounces (340 g) feta cheese
2 tablespoons unsalted butter, melted

PROTEIN
1 large egg

PANTRY
Kosher salt and freshly ground black pepper
Extra-virgin oil

FREEZER
13 sheets (14 by 18 inches/35 by 45 cm each) fresh or frozen (thawed) phyllo dough

Prep the veggies: Finely chop 1 pound (454 g) baby spinach and add to a large bowl. Finely chop ½ yellow onion, ½ cup (15 g) chopped dill, ½ cup (16 g) chopped parsley, and 6 green onions (white and green parts), and add to the bowl with the spinach.

Lightly beat 1 egg and add to the bowl. Crumble 12 ounces (340 g) feta and zest 2 lemons directly into the bowl. Season with ½ teaspoon salt and freshly ground pepper. Mix well, massaging the spinach, to combine.

Assemble and bake the spanakopita: Preheat the oven to 375°F (190°C). Drizzle a 10-inch (25 cm) cast-iron skillet with a little olive oil. Add 1 sheet of phyllo and drizzle or brush a little bit more oil on top. Repeat with 4 more sheets of phyllo, alternating the direction of the sheets each time to cover the entire bottom of the skillet.

Add the filling and repeat the layering process with 5 sheets of phyllo. Then gather the edges and flop them over and kind of scrunch them around the border like a traditional pie crust. Then crumple the remaining 3 pieces of phyllo like little softballs and put them on top, filling in the flat part of the crust. Brush with 2 tablespoons melted butter. (You don't have to use butter here; you can use olive oil, but I like the flavor.) Score the pie into 8 slices, not cutting all the way through.

Bake until the top is golden brown, 40 to 45 minutes. Wait at least 10 minutes before cutting and serving.

Stuffed Artichoke with Breadcrumbs and So Much Garlic

Makes 4

This one gives me *Moosewood Cookbook* vibes, ultimate vegetarian comfort food. Moosewood, and of course my Grandpa Pat, who used to make big stuffed artichokes with tons of garlic.

PRODUCE
4 lemons
4 large artichokes
8 cloves garlic
2 bunches parsley, chopped, stems reserved
  separately

DAIRY
1 cup (100 g) grated Parmesan cheese

PANTRY
2 cups (140 g) Basic Breadcrumbs (page 265)
Extra-virgin olive oil
Kosher salt and freshly ground pepper

Prep the artichokes: Preheat the oven to 400°F (205°C).

Cut 1 lemon in half and squeeze its juice into a large bowl of water, then throw in the spent lemon halves.

Trim 4 artichokes, working with one at a time. Snap off the tough outer bottom leaves. Use a serrated knife to cut off the upper third of the artichoke. Snip the remaining leaf tips with scissors. Trim the long stem, leaving a flat bottom. Gently spread the artichoke leaves away from the center, revealing the choke. Remove the choke with a spoon and discard. Place

the artichoke in the lemon water. Repeat with the remaining artichokes.

Make the filling: In a medium bowl, combine 2 cups (140 g) breadcrumbs, 1 cup (100 g) grated Parmesan, a little drizzle of oil, 2 bunches chopped parsley, and the zest from 2 of the remaining lemons. Season with salt and pepper.

Remove the artichokes from the water and drain well. Fill each artichoke with ¼ of the breadcrumb mixture; spread the leaves to allow the stuffing to sit inside, and mound some stuffing on top.

Bake the artichokes and serve: Place 1 inch (2.5 cm) of water in the bottom of a 9 by 9-inch (23 by 23 cm) baking dish or a Dutch oven. Throw in the lemons that you zested and the parsley stems, and add a good amount of salt. Fit the artichokes into the baking dish. Drizzle with 2 tablespoons oil. Cover tightly with aluminum foil. Bake until the heart is soft when pierced with the tip of a knife, 45 to 50 minutes. Remove the foil and bake until the breadcrumbs are golden brown, about 10 minutes more. Cut the remaining lemon into wedges and serve them on the side.

California Sprout Sandwich

Makes 2

There is nothing like a California veggie sandwich. Maybe it's just because it's the salad of sandwiches, but I think it's perfect. Almost every LA lunch spot seems to have its own version today, but they all have one thing in common—sprouts. According to Jonathan Kauffman, who wrote the book *Hippie Food*, until the 1970s only Southern Californians ate alfalfa sprouts. This one is based on the Source's open-faced veggie sandwich—but you can add other veggies for additional crunch if you've got 'em—grated carrots, cucumbers . . . why not?

PRODUCE
1 lemon
¼ cup (15 g) loosely packed mixed fresh herbs,
  such as chives, parsley, and dill
1 avocado
½ red onion
1 cup (60 g) alfalfa or broccoli sprouts

DAIRY
2 slices sharp cheddar cheese

PANTRY
¼ cup (60 ml) mayonnaise (or Vegenaise)
Kosher salt and freshly ground black pepper
4 thick slices whole-wheat bread
Salt and freshly ground black pepper

Make the dressing: In a small bowl, mix together the zest and juice of 1 lemon, ¼ cup (60 ml) mayonnaise, and ¼ cup (15 g) assorted herbs. Season to taste with salt and pepper.

Prep the vegetables: Slice the avocado and ½ red onion.

Assemble the sandwiches: Slather the dressing on all 4 slices whole-wheat bread. Pile each sandwich high with half the cheese, red onion, avocado, and sprouts and serve.

Orecchiette with Roasted Cherry Tomato Sauce

Serves 4

When I worked for Martha (Stewart), Sarah (Carey) made a recipe like this for *Everyday Food*, and now it's how I make tomato sauce 95 percent of the time. It takes a little more time than opening a jar of marinara and heating it up, but cherry tomatoes are always available and it's worth the minor effort. This sauce is bright, a little sweet, and a nice way to make pasta for one. It also tastes great on zoodles.

PRODUCE
3 cloves garlic
2 pints (580 g) cherry tomatoes

DAIRY
Freshly grated Parmesan cheese, for serving

PANTRY
2 anchovies
3 glugs extra-virgin olive oil
Kosher salt
Red pepper flakes
1 pound (454 g) orecchiette pasta

Prep: Preheat the oven to 450°F (230ºC). Thinly slice 3 cloves garlic. Give 2 anchovies a good chop.

Cook the sauce: On a parchment-lined rimmed baking sheet, toss 2 pints (580 g) cherry tomatoes, the sliced garlic, a good pinch red pepper flakes, and 3 glugs olive oil together to combine. Season with salt and add more oil if it looks dry—don't be afraid, you're making a sauce. Roast until the tomatoes are bursting and browned, 25 to 30 minutes.

Meanwhile, cook the pasta and serve: Cook the orecchiette according to the package instructions. Reserve 1 cup (240 ml) pasta water before draining. Drain and return to the pot along with the roasted tomatoes. Add a bit of pasta water at a time, starting with about ¼ cup (60 ml), and stir so that the tomatoes continue to break down a bit and their juices cling to the pasta. Add a bit more pasta water if necessary. Serve with Parmesan cheese, if desired.

Vegan Mushroom Lasagna

Serves 8

This recipe drove me crazy when I was trying to get it just right, but I felt compelled to make a delicious vegan lasagna that does not use store-bought vegan cheese. I am not vegan, but I am lactose intolerant, and while I do occasionally indulge in cheese, I should not. I hate that so many of the nondairy products out there are full of coconut oil, gums, and I don't even know what. This uses every single hippie trick in the book (tofu ricotta, nutritional yeast, apple cider vinegar, miso) and it came together to make something that is not exactly like traditional lasagna but is so good. It's its own special thing for people who can't eat cheese to enjoy.

PRODUCE

2 pounds (910 g) mixed mushrooms, such as cremini, shiitake, and maitake
2 cloves garlic
1 large yellow onion
1 lemon
Handful fresh basil leaves

PROTEIN

1 (14-ounce/397 g) block extra-firm tofu

PANTRY

1 cup (115 g) walnuts, toasted (see page 33)
Extra-virgin olive oil
Kosher salt and freshly ground black pepper
¼ cup (60 ml) tomato paste
2 cups (472 ml) Umami Mushroom Stock (page 270)
1 tablespoon white miso
1 head Roasted Garlic (page 269)
3 cups (720 ml) cashew milk, store-bought or homemade (see page 266)
¼ cup (30 g) tapioca starch
2 tablespoons nutritional yeast
1 tablespoon apple cider vinegar
12 lasagna noodles

Prep: Preheat the oven to 400°F (205°C) with a rack in the upper position. Finely crush 1 cup (115 g) toasted walnuts and set aside.

Meanwhile, prep the veggies: Use a food processor to give 2 pounds (910 g) mushrooms a good chop if you have one, or use a knife to finely chop in a few batches. Mince 2 cloves garlic and 1 onion.

Make the mushroom sauce: Heat a large deep-sided skillet over medium-high. Add about ¼ cup (60 ml) olive oil and the onion. Cook until the edges of the onion begin to turn deep brown, but not burnt, about 10 minutes. Lower the heat to medium and continue to cook, adding a little water to the pan if the onions dry out to prevent burning, until they are incredibly soft and fully caramelized, about 20 minutes. Stir in the walnuts.

Add the minced garlic to the pan, cook for 1 minute, and then add the chopped mushrooms. Cook until they release all their liquid, about 15 minutes. Season generously with salt and pepper and add ¼ cup (60 ml) tomato paste. Cook for about 2 minutes, and then add 2 cups mushroom stock. Cook for about 10 minutes,

(Continued)

until the sauce has reduced a bit. Taste and adjust the seasoning.

Make the "ricotta": Combine one 14-ounce (397 g) block extra-firm tofu, the juice of ½ lemon, and 1 tablespoon miso in a food processor. Blend until very smooth. Add a handful of basil leaves and a good amount of salt and pepper and blend again, then taste for seasoning.

Make the "mozzarella": Squeeze 1 head roasted garlic into a small saucepan and then add 3 cups (720 ml) cashew milk. Whisk in ¼ cup (30 g) tapioca starch, 2 tablespoons nutritional yeast, and 1 tablespoon apple cider vinegar. Season well with salt and pepper. Keep on a low, low heat and stir occasionally—try to use as soon as possible; the mixture will thicken as it sits.

Assemble the lasagna: Boil 12 lasagna noodles according to the package instructions.

In a 10-inch (25 cm) skillet, add some of the mushroom sauce as the bottom layer, so the noodles won't stick to the pan, and then top with 3 noodles. Top the noodles with one-third of the mushroom sauce, then one-third of the "ricotta" mixture, and a dollop of "mozzarella." Repeat 2 more times. For the last layer, top with 3 more noodles and the remaining "mozzarella."

Bake and serve: Cover with parchment-lined foil and bake for 25 minutes. Uncover and set your oven to broil. Broil until the "mozzarella" starts to brown in places, about 2 minutes. Allow the lasagna to cool for 10 to 15 minutes before cutting and serving.

Creamy Corn and Zucchini Pasta with Basil and Pine Nuts

Serves 4

Call it a sauce or a dressing. Blending sweet corn kernels with a little olive oil and basil might as well be called alchemy because it becomes liquid gold. And it comes together in minutes. It can be quite sweet with in-season corn, so make sure to add Parmesan or Pecorino to keep it savory.

....

PRODUCE
3 ears sweet corn
2 large zucchini (about 14 ounces/400 g)
3 cloves garlic
1 lemon
Big handful fresh basil leaves, plus more for
  serving

DAIRY
¼ cup (25 g) grated Parmesan or Pecorino cheese,
  plus more for serving

PANTRY
¼ cup (60 ml) extra-virgin olive oil, plus more for
  drizzling
Kosher salt and freshly ground black pepper
12 ounces (340 g) spaghetti
½ cup (70 g) pine nuts, toasted (see page 33)
Pinch crushed red pepper flakes (optional)

Prep the produce: Bring a large pot of salted water to a boil. Working confidently, stand 1 ear of corn on a rimmed baking sheet, and cut down the side of the corn to remove the kernels. Repeat with the other 2 ears.

Use a julienne peeler or a spiralizer to cut 2 zucchini into "noodles." Zest and then juice 1 lemon.

Make the sauce: Transfer the corn kernels to a blender with 3 cloves garlic, 1/4 cup (60 ml) oil, juice of ½ lemon, and a big pinch of salt and pepper. Blend, blend, blend until very smooth. Add a big handful of basil and blend again until it's finely chopped.

Cook the pasta: Add 12 ounces (340 g) spaghetti to the boiling water. Cook the pasta according to the package instructions. Reserve about 1 cup (240 ml) pasta water, then drain the pasta and return it to the pot.

Add ¼ cup (60 ml) of the pasta water to the pasta pot, along with the zucchini and the corn mixture. Turn the heat on to medium and cook until just warmed through. Taste for seasoning.

Assemble and serve: Serve the pasta with additional basil leaves, ½ cup (70 g) pine nuts, and a *litttttle* more Parm. Add a pinch of crushed red pepper flakes and lemon zest, if desired.

Trumpet Mushrooms with Soba Noodles, Soy, and Butter

Serves 2 to 4

These simple flavors feel elegant, and they come together to create a vegetarian dish that feels incredibly rich. Toss in some of your favorite greens if you want, but the depth of this dish's savory, toasty nuttiness is something I didn't want to mess with. Other mushrooms work just as well, but I like the texture of trumpets here in contrast to the noodles.

. . . .

<u>PRODUCE</u>
1 pound (454 g) trumpet mushrooms
2 cloves garlic

<u>DAIRY</u>
6 tablespoons (85 g) unsalted butter

<u>PANTRY</u>
8 ounces (226 g) soba noodles
2 tablespoons soy sauce

Prep the mushrooms: Trim off the ends off 1 pound (454 g) trumpet mushrooms and, using either a knife or a mandoline, carefully slice or shave the mushrooms into thin strips (about the thickness of two coins).

Cook the noodles and the mushrooms: Set a medium pot of water to boil over high heat. Boil 8 ounces (226 g) soba according to the package instructions. Rinse the cooked noodles with water so they don't stick together.

In a large skillet or wok, heat 2 tablespoons of the butter and add half the mushrooms. Let them sit undisturbed for about 3 minutes, flip when the mushrooms are beautifully golden brown, and cook 3 minutes more, adding a bit more butter if necessary. Repeat with 2 more tablespoons butter and the rest of the mushrooms.

Assemble and serve: Return the rest of the mushrooms to the pan, add 2 tablespoons soy and 2 tablespoons butter, and swirl everything around to combine. Add the soba noodles, toss, and serve.

Broccoli Pasta with Peas and Pecorino

Serves 4

Broccoli has always been one of my favorite foods, so this one is heavy on the broccoli. It's not hiding the vegetables, but there are a lot more vegetables in here than you might guess—it's really getting your greens in for the day. This has been a big hit with (even picky) kiddos. Swap nutritional yeast for the cheese if you're vegan!

PRODUCE
1 head broccoli (with stems)
2 handfuls fresh basil leaves
2 handfuls baby spinach leaves
2 cloves garlic
2 lemons

PANTRY
1 (14-ounce/400 g) can white beans
¼ cup (25 g) grated Pecorino Romano or Parmesan cheese, plus more for serving
Extra-virgin olive oil
Kosher salt and freshly ground black pepper
1 pound (454 g) whole-wheat or chickpea rigatoni
Crushed red pepper flakes (optional)

FREEZER
1 cup (158 g) frozen peas

Bring a large pot of heavily salted water to a boil. Prepare an ice bath by filling a large bowl with ice water.

Prep the veggies: Trim the broccoli into florets, and cut the stems into ¼-inch (6 mm) thick pieces.

Prep the pesto: Drop 2 handfuls basil and 2 handfuls baby spinach into the boiling water, just until wilted and bright green, which only takes a few seconds. Transfer the leaves to the ice bath to cool.

Put 1 cup (158 g) peas in a fine-mesh strainer and give them a dunk in the boiling water for 1 minute, and then add them to a food processor. Add the broccoli and garlic to the pot and cook until bright green, 5 to 7 minutes, then carefully transfer the broccoli to the food processor.

Gently squeeze a little bit of water out of the spinach and basil and add the leaves to the food processor.

Blend the pesto: Drain and rinse one 14-ounce (400 g) can white beans and add them to the food processor along with ¼ cup (25 g) cheese and a little drizzle of olive oil, zest and juice from 2 lemons, and a good sprinkle of salt. Process until smooth. Taste for seasoning.

Cook the pasta: Add 1 pound (454 g) rigatoni to the boiling water and cook according to the package instructions. Reserve about 1 cup (240 ml) of the cooking liquid, then drain. Return the pasta to the pot along with the pesto and about ¼ cup (60 ml) of the pasta water. Add more pasta water as needed to create a smooth sauce that coats the pasta.

Serve: Top with additional cheese and red pepper flakes, if desired.

Steamed Clams in Sweet Pepper and Corn Broth

Serves 2 to 4 as a light meal

I haven't traveled much over the past couple of years; I have been very busy writing books. But I have gotten to travel a bit for tours and one of my favorite stops was Seattle. I went to the Walrus and the Carpenter two nights in a row when they had an amazing clam special with a sweet yellow pepper that I'll never remember the name of—but yellow wax peppers, or a delicious sweet pepper from the farmer's market like a Jimmy Nardello, work well. Corn flavors the broth so quickly here and ties the whole thing together.

PRODUCE
3 ears corn
4 sweet peppers (7 ounces/200 g), such as yellow wax peppers or Jimmy Nardello
4 cloves garlic
1 lemon

DAIRY
2 tablespoons unsalted butter

PROTEIN
2 pounds (908 g) small clams, such as littlenecks or Manila

PANTRY
Extra-virgin olive oil
Crushed red pepper flakes
Kosher salt and freshly ground black pepper
¾ cup (6 ounces/177 ml) dry white wine
Crusty bread, toasted, for serving

Prep the veggies: Working confidently, stand 1 ear of corn in a rimmed baking sheet and cut down the side of the cob to remove the kernels. Repeat with the other 2 ears. Trim the stem and remove the seeds from 4 sweet peppers and thinly slice into rings. Thinly slice 4 cloves garlic.

Cook the clams: Heat a straight-sided skillet over medium heat and drizzle with a good glug of olive oil. Once it starts to shimmer, add the garlic. You want the garlic to get very nice and golden, not too dark, so adjust the heat as needed. Add the sliced peppers, red pepper flakes, and 2 tablespoons butter. Cook until the peppers begin to soften a bit, about 5 minutes. Season with a bit of salt and pepper. Add the corn, 2 pounds (908 g) clams, and ¾ cup (177 ml) wine, and cover the pan.

Cook until all the little clams open up; this can start happening immediately or take 6 to 8 minutes, depending on the clams, but if it goes on longer than this and they are sealed shut, toss them!

Season and serve: Taste the sauce for seasoning. Squeeze in a little lemon juice. Spoon the sauce and clams into serving bowls.

Serve with bread—and with a bit of olive oil. You'll want more than one slice to sop up the sauce.

Sheet-Pan Salmon with Green Beans, Potatoes, Olives, and Spicy Tahini

Serves 4

Roasted green beans are so much more exciting when they still have a good crisp, that almost fried texture, to them. Dinner is so much more exciting when you have only one pan to clean up when it's all done. This is a combination of a lot of my favorite things. It's super satisfying, extremely easy, and a great go-to for dinner parties where you want to spend less time in the kitchen.

....

PRODUCE
1 pound (454 g) baby Yukon gold potatoes
2 lemons
8 ounces (226 g) green beans

PROTEIN
4 (4- to 6-ounce/115 to 170 g) salmon or steelhead trout fillets

PANTRY
Extra-virgin olive oil
Kosher salt and freshly ground black pepper
½ cup (100 g) Cerignola olives
1 recipe Spicy Tahini (page 276)
¼ cup (60 g) pistachios, toasted (see page 33)

Preheat the oven to 425°F (220°C).

Prep the veggies: Cut 1 pound (454 g) baby potatoes and 2 lemons in half and transfer to a bowl. Toss with a good drizzle of olive oil, season well with salt and pepper, and arrange the potatoes and lemon halves on the baking sheet, cut side down. Trim the ends off 8 ounces (226 g) green beans.

Cook the veggies: Roast the potatoes and lemons until beginning to turn golden, 20 to 25 minutes. Give the potatoes a little shake and remove the pan from the oven.

Cook the fish and serve: Season four 4- to 6-ounce (115 to 170 g) salmon fillets generously with salt and pepper. Add to the pan along with the potatoes. Use the same bowl you tossed the potatoes in to toss the green beans with some oil and a little salt and pepper. Add to the pan, making sure everything in the pan has a little room to breathe.

Roast until the salmon is cooked through, about 20 minutes more. Toss ½ cup (100 g) olives with the potatoes and green beans. Drizzle with spicy tahini and sprinkle with ¼ cup (60 g) pistachios and serve.

WHY DO I HAVE A FAVORITE RECIPE OF RAM DASS IN THIS BOOK?

If you are wondering why, I think the best place to start is by viewing page 15 of his book *Be Here Now*, where you'll see a drawing of a man who looks very much like my partner, Ben, looking into a mirror. Although the square blue book had been sitting in my childhood home forever, and I had flipped through the pages many times, it wasn't until Ben noticed this resemblance that RD took on a new importance, and a pull on my life.

If you're not familiar with RD and his work, let me give you the abbreviated biography. Ram Dass, who was born as Richard Alpert in 1931, was a Harvard professor and pioneer of the psychedelic movement of the 1960s. He flew Cessnas, and drove motorcycles and Mercedes, and met his soul on mushrooms, but was fired from Harvard for giving psychedelics to a minor early in his career. Alpert went to India in 1967, and after an encounter with Neem Karoli Baba, aka Maharaj-ji, he returned to the United States as Baba Ram Dass. He began lecturing, offering Westerners an extremely human, honest, humble, and humorous approach to spirituality. In 1971 he published *Be Here Now*, the blue book mentioned above.

Ben had already been researching RD, and driving up the coast of California in his VW van, doing a lot of LSD and paddleboarding and listening to his lectures, when I moved to LA. Once I was there, we kept listening, and driving, and paddleboarding. In 2021 I surprised him with a trip to Maui for his birthday, the place where Ram Dass spent the final decades of life. A quick Google search brought me to the local Maui newspaper's obituary for RD, where a photo of him — completely blissed out, doing his weekly float at his secret spot with his friends and caretakers — led me to Mike Crall, who would eventually set up a whole odyssey for us.

The end was the perfect place to begin. I got behind the wheel of the familiar but much more worn-out, rusted-up Vanagon I had rented and drove through Haiku with the windows down. It was all breeze and palm trees and lush green on the way to the Death Store. Ben didn't know where we were going, but on the drive, he told me he had been thinking about death all morning. We walked through the shelves of hamburger-shaped urns, biodegradable caskets, and books about dying to find Reverend Bodhi Be, a smiling rebel Sufi teacher, off-grid homesteader, tropical-fruit farmer, and death and grief educator who had started the shop and organization with his wife and Ram Dass in 2012. It was the Maui chapter of Ram Dass's story that intrigued me more than the psychedelic Harvard days with Timothy Leary — the final chapter of his life, really, when he softened, and surrendered to and truly embodied the love he had been talking about and teaching his whole life.

While so much of this story feels like it's Ben's to tell — I don't know what chunks to put in or what I'm leaving out — I don't feel as though I've just been along for the ride. Since that trip to Maui, I've had the opportunity to meet an entire community of seekers, misfits, musicians, and philosophers, and just a lot of new faces and souls. Some of RD's caretakers have come and stayed for weeks at a time at our home over the past couple of years, cracking our open-door policy even farther open, and getting into the "heart cave," in RD-speak. And this has expanded to others; there is always someone at our house, or coming, or going.

The story that is mine, and continues to be mine, is learning to soften too. Into myself. I know all RD's tricks. Being open, being funny, admitting my flaws — that is all easy after reading the books of his that I have. Learning to lean into life instead of pushing forward, how to release, let go, surrender, to float. To not call those things the work that needs to be done, but instead let them happen. To stop using my brain and live out of my heart. Neurotic Jewish men have always been my biggest weakness; but, RD and BS, you're breaking me open.

To let someone see all your strangeness, and your ugliness, and your beauty. Your strengths and weaknesses and everything you have been and wish you could be, all at once. To let yourself just be all those things. To sit in this bag of bones and let your soul rip and be able to laugh about it. Well, it's just about the scariest and most thrilling thing you can do. Sure, a little bit of that happens every time you create. Every book, painting, sculpture, whatever it is — it's all out there for the world to see, too. But to forget about it as a story and just be there with somebody on this planet for a while . . .

Ram Dass's Slow-Roasted Salmon with Passion Fruit

Serves 4 as a meal

Gillian Adamo cooked for Ram Dass in Maui from 2015 to 2019 and I'm so grateful that she shared this beautiful recipe for one of his favorite dishes. Lilikoi, or passion fruit, grows in Hawaii and California and is available online from growers such as Rincon Tropics, or you can find frozen pulp in many grocery stores. The flavor is tart and sweet, and it creates a luscious sauce with the rich coconut oil and touch of honey. But blood oranges can be used as a substitute. Gillian would serve this to RD with a salad and grilled asparagus—I love it with the Big Green Gingery Salad on page 160.

PRODUCE
4 green onions
2 cloves garlic
2 passion fruit or ½ cup (120 ml) blood orange juice plus 1 whole blood orange
Handful Thai basil

PROTEIN
4 (4- to 6-ounce/115 to 170 g) wild salmon fillets

PANTRY
Kosher salt
3 tablespoons coconut oil
1 tablespoon honey
Tamari sauce
Flaky salt (or black lava salt if you can find it!)

Prep the produce and fish: Heat an outdoor grill to 250ºF (120ºC) or the oven to 350ºF (175ºC). Thinly slice the light green and whites of 4 green onions. Thinly slice 2 cloves garlic. If using passion fruit, cut them in half and scoop out fleshy fruity insides and put them in a bowl (you should have roughly ¾ cup (4 g) fruit). If using a blood orange instead, slice the orange into 8 thin slices

Pat the salmon dry and season generously with salt.

Assemble the packets: Arrange 4 parchment-lined sheets of aluminum foil (or just parchment if you will be using the oven) on the counter.

Lay a few plops of passion fruit or 2 slices blood orange in the center of each piece of parchment. Place a salmon fillet onto the fruit.

Drizzle each fillet with coconut oil and a little bit of honey. Sprinkle the green onions and garlic slices over the fillets.

If using passion fruit, take a spoon and spoon more sweet, juicy fruit over the fillets. If using blood orange juice, pour 2 tablespoons (30 ml) over each fillet. Splash a little bit of tamari on each fillet.

Seal the packets by folding the parchment rectangles in half over the fish and crimping the edges together, sealing them tightly and leaving enough room in the packets for the fish to steam.

Cook and serve: Grill or roast the packets until the fish is cooked through, 25 to 30 minutes, but this could vary slightly depending on the thickness of your salmon fillets. Carefully open the packets and serve sprinkled with Thai basil and flaky salt.

Halibut with Sungolds, Fennel, and Saffron

Serves 4

En papillote means *in paper*, and it's a great way to cook fish indoors if you're afraid your house or apartment will smell like fish, or if you're afraid of cooking fish in general. It is also incredibly healthy; since it's steamed, the only fat that you need to add is for a bit of flavor. It's a self-saucing dish—all you have to do is put everything together in little paper packets and it basically cooks itself. I like to assemble the packets beforehand, keep them in the fridge, and then pop them in the oven when I'm just about ready to serve. Cooking in parchment is so easy, and so versatile, I hope you are inspired to try your own combinations with seasonal ingredients as well. See page 223 for another way to put this technique to use.

PRODUCE
1 small head fennel
1½ pounds (680 g) Sungolds or other sweet
 cherry tomato
1 lemon

DAIRY
4 tablespoons (55 g) unsalted butter

PROTEIN
1¼ pounds (570 g) or 4 (6-ounce/170 g) striped
 bass, cod, or halibut fillets, skin removed

PANTRY
Extra-virgin olive oil
Kosher salt and freshly ground black pepper
Pinch saffron

Preheat the oven to 450°F (230°C).

Prep the veggies: To thinly and evenly slice 1 head fennel, I recommend cutting it in half and then slicing it whisper thin on a mandoline. Slice 1½ pounds (680 g) cherry tomatoes in half. Thinly slice the lemon.

Assemble the packets: For each of the four packets, you'll need roughly a 20-inch-long (50 cm) piece of parchment paper. I order pre-cut parchment sheets that are half-sheet-pan size online because I'm lazy, and I like the sheets to be flat because they are easier to deal with. And those sheets are perfect here. Fold your sheet of parchment in half like a book. Open it up, and on one side of the crease, build up your little pile. Start with one-quarter of the fennel and tomatoes, then drizzle with a little oil, and season with salt and pepper. Place one 6-ounce (170 g) piece of fish on top. Season with salt and pepper and sprinkle with a pinch of saffron. Top with a few very thin slices of lemon and 1 tablespoon butter. Repeat with the remaining packets.

To seal the packets, fold the top half over the fish, and make small overlapping folds to close the edges. Store the packets for up to a day in the fridge, until you are ready to cook.

Cook the fish: When you're ready to cook the fish, arrange the packets on 2 sheet pans, and place them in a the preheated oven. Roast them until the parchment paper is puffed, about 12 minutes. If you allow guests to open their own packets, warn them that there will be hot steam!

Health Nut

Steamed Bass with Tokyo Turnips, Ginger, Soy, and Green Onion

Serves 4

When I traveled to Japan, my first stop was Okinawa because I really wanted to surf. I didn't surf, because it rained most of the time, but I did spend a lot of time at the market. I don't speak any Japanese and I love communicating through gestures and trying new things that are completely mysterious. The first meal, and maybe the most delicious thing I had while in Japan, was an "uncle fish" steamed in a simple ginger, garlic, and green onion broth. Uncle fish are pretty hard to come by in the United States, but any fillet of flaky white fish, like black bass, or red snapper, is beautiful here. If you can't find tender white baby turnips, feel free to swap them with snow peas, baby bok choy, or thinly sliced bok choy, enoki mushrooms, or even sliced shiitakes. This is a different, more evergreen variation of the same cooking technique as on page 220. Cooking in parchment is so easy, and so versatile, I hope you are inspired to try your own combinations with seasonal ingredients as well.

....

PRODUCE
1 bunch Tokyo turnips, halved, with greens
2-inch (5 cm) piece fresh ginger, peeled and chopped
6 green onions, white and green parts, chopped

DAIRY
4 tablespoons (½ stick/55 g) unsalted butter

PROTEIN
1 pound (454 g) black sea bass, cut into 4 fillets

PANTRY
4 teaspoons soy sauce
Kosher salt and freshly ground black pepper
Drizzle of toasted sesame oil (optional)

Assemble the packets: For each of the four packets, you'll need roughly a 20-inch-long (50 cm) piece of parchment paper. I order pre-cut parchment sheets that are half-sheet-pan size online because I'm lazy, and I like the sheets to be flat because they are easier to deal with. And those sheets are perfect here. Fold your sheet of parchment in half like a book. Open it up, and on one side of the crease, build up a little pile. Start with one-quarter of the turnips and greens, then one-quarter of the ginger, green onions, and soy sauce. Place 1 fish fillet on top. Season with salt and pepper and top with 1 tablespoon butter. Repeat with the remaining packets.

To seal the packets, fold the top half over the fish, and make small overlapping folds to close the edges. Store the packets for up to 24 hours in the fridge, until you are ready to cook.

When you're ready to cook, preheat the oven to 450°F (230°C).

Cook the fish: Arrange the packets on 2 sheet pans and roast them until the parchment paper is puffed, about 12 minutes. If you allow guests to open their own packets, warn them that there will be hot steam! Invite them to drizzle their fish with a little sesame oil, if they wish.

Roasted Cauliflower Flatbreads with Spicy Tahini and Sumac Onions

Serves 4

Michael Solomonov, the co-owner and chef of the influential Israeli restaurant Zahav in Philadelphia, made my friend Benny Blanco an amazing lamb shawarma recipe for the book we wrote together, *Open Wide*, and it really inspired me to make a vegetarian version of a deliciously spiced pita sandwich. This also makes a great bowl over greens.

PRODUCE
1 small red onion
1 lemon
2 large heads cauliflower
Handful fresh mint
Handful fresh cilantro

PANTRY
2 tablespoons ground turmeric
1 tablespoon ground cumin
2 teaspoons garlic powder
1 teaspoon freshly ground black pepper
½ teaspoon ground cinnamon
Kosher salt
2 teaspoons sumac
Extra-virgin olive oil
4 store-bought whole-wheat naan breads
Fennel Tzatziki (page 143)
Spicy Tahini (page 276)

Preheat the oven to 425°F (220°C).

Make the spice blend: In a large bowl, combine 2 tablespoons turmeric, 1 tablespoon ground cumin, 2 teaspoons garlic powder, 1 teaspoon black pepper, ½ teaspoon cinnamon, and a good pinch of salt.

Prep the onion: Thinly slice 1 small red onion. Sprinkle with a bit of salt and the juice of 1 lemon. Sprinkle with 2 teaspoons sumac and let sit while you cook, stirring occationally.

Make the cauliflower: Remove the core and cut the cauliflowers into florets. Toss in the bowl with the spice mix and a good glug of olive oil. The turmeric will stain your hands (and literally everything in your kitchen), so wear gloves or use tongs! Transfer to 2 rimmed baking sheets and sprinkle with salt. Roast until deep golden brown in spots, about 25 minutes.

Assemble and serve the flatbreads: Carefully, with the burner on medium-high, place the naan, one at a time, directly on the flame for a few seconds per side to warm it up and char it a little bit.

Spread a bit of tzatziki on each naan, then top with the roasted cauliflower, onions, spicy tahini, a squeeze of lemon, a dusting of sumac, and some fresh mint and cilantro.

Avocado Summer Rolls

Makes 10 rolls

Rice paper wrappers are a little tricky to handle at first, but once you get the rolling down, there are kind-of-endless possibilities for what you can put inside for a quick meal. I love these as lunch or dinner. I find them super satisfying, especially with a rich and creamy sauce like the spicy green goddess dressing (see page 180) or the spicy peanut sauce (see page 133). Jicama has a mild, sweet flavor and incredible crunch and makes the addition of rice noodles unnecessary.

....

PRODUCE
1 head Bibb or butter lettuce, leaves separated
1 bunch fresh basil
1 small jicama
4 Persian cucumbers or 1 English cucumber
2 avocados
1 lime
2 handfuls broccoli or alfalfa sprouts

PROTEIN
1 (14-ounce/397 g) block firm tofu

PANTRY
1 tablespoon vegetable oil
Kosher salt
2 tablespoons cornstarch
1 (12-ounce/340 g) package rice paper spring
   roll wrappers
Spicy green goddess dressing (page 180) or spicy
   peanut sauce (page 133)

Preheat the oven to 425°F (220°C).

Prep the tofu: Press one 14-ounce (397 g) block tofu using a tofu press or cut the tofu lengthwise into five pieces and press using paper towels or clean dish towels and a heavy pan for at least 20 minutes.

Cook the tofu: If you've used a tofu press, cut the pressed block into 5 (¾-inch/2 cm) rectangles.

Cut the tofu crosswise into ten ¾-inch-thick (2 cm) strips. Transfer the strips to a rimmed baking sheet. Toss with oil and season very generously with salt. Sprinkle with the cornstarch and toss again. Bake until golden brown and very crispy, about 25 to 30 minutes, flipping at least once halfway through.

Prep the veggies: Separate the leaves of 1 head lettuce and make sure they are clean and dry. Remove 1 bunch basil leaves from their stems. Peel and julienne 1 jicama (using a julienne peeler!) or cut into matchsticks with a knife. Julienne 4 cucumbers. Slice 2 avocados and give them a squeeze of lime juice to prevent the avocado from oxidizing.

Assemble the rolls: Working one at a time, dip a spring roll wrapper in a baking dish filled with warm water until it is just pliable, about 15 seconds. Place some basil leaves in a row, then top with a lettuce leaf. Fill the leaf with jicama, cucumber, a piece of fried tofu, sprouts, and avocado slices.

Roll it up like a burrito, starting by folding in the shorter sides, and then rolling up the summer roll into a tight cigar. Enjoy with spicy green goddess dressing or spicy peanut sauce.

Shiitake and Broccoli Stir-Fry

Serves 2

In my life I have probably made thousands of stir-fries. In college I'm pretty sure I survived off Trader Joe's frozen stir-fry vegetables alone. While the combinations of ingredients are endless, this has become my go-to. It feels very fresh, healthy, and substantial; there is plenty of crunch and texture; it's earthy, sweet, salty, and just perfectly balanced. Plus, all these veggies have a pretty long life span in the fridge drawer. The prep doesn't take much more time than reaching for your freezer, and it is *so much better*.

PRODUCE
8 ounces (225 g) shiitake mushrooms
1 head broccoli
½ head red cabbage
4 carrots
2-inch (5 cm) piece fresh ginger, peeled and cut into matchsticks
1 bunch green onions, or ½ red onion

PROTEIN
1 (14-ounce/397 g) block extra-firm tofu

PANTRY
Kosher salt
Neutral oil, such as sunflower or avocado, or coconut oil
2 tablespoons tamari
2 teaspoons sesame oil
Gomasio (see page 28), your favorite hot sauce, and/or kimchi for serving
Cooked brown rice (see page 268), for serving

Prep the tofu: Press one 14-ounce (397 g) block tofu using a tofu press or cut the tofu lengthwise into five pieces and press using paper towels or clean dish towels and a heavy pan for at least 20 minutes. If you've used a tofu press, cut the pressed block lengthwise into 5 pieces. Cut the tofu crosswise into ¾-inch (2 cm) rectangles and season with a bit of salt.

Prep the veggies: Thinly slice 8 ounces (225 g) shiitake mushrooms. Cut 1 head broccoli into small florets. Use a knife or a mandoline to shave ½ head red cabbage into ⅛-inch (3 mm) strips. Cut 4 carrots into matchsticks with a julienne peeler or a knife. Peel and cut a 2-inch (5 cm) piece ginger into matchsticks. Thinly slice 1 bunch green onions, keeping the whites and greens separate.

Cook the vegetables and tofu: Heat a large skillet or wok over medium-high heat. Add some oil, and once it's shimmering, add the tofu. Cook, without moving, until the tofu easily unsticks from the pan, about 5 minutes. Flip and cook for 5 minutes more. Transfer the tofu to a plate.

Add the mushrooms to the pan and cook, until they have released all their liquid and are golden brown on at least one side, about 5 minutes.

Add a little oil if the pan is too dry, and then add the broccoli and cabbage and cook, stirring occasionally, until just tender. Add the carrots, ginger, and the whites of the green onions and cook until fragrant and tender.

Add the tofu back into the pan. Add 3 tablespoons tamari and 2 teaspoons sesame oil and the green parts of the green onion and toss.

Season and serve: Taste for seasoning and serve over the brown rice. Add some gomasio, your favorite hot sauce, and/or kimchi for extra seasoning or a little spice.

Vegan "Tuna" or Chickpea Salad Collard-Green Wraps

Serves 2

When I was developing the recipes for this book, Ben was recording an album with some friends in our music studio. The boys made great recipe testers. When my friend Johnny Moods (guitars and vocals in the band), who was traveling from Berlin, first tried a collard green wrap from Erewhon, his mind was completely blown and he said I had to make this for the book. So here it is! A collard green wrap with my favorite super-savory vegan filling—protein-packed chickpea salad, or "tuna," which my friend Jason always tries to sell it as. It may not sound like much, but it's truly addicting.

PRODUCE
1 lemon
2 large collard green leaves
1 Persian cucumber
½ small red onion (60 g)
1 cup (90 g) broccoli or alfalfa sprouts

PANTRY
1 (14-ounce/400 g) can chickpeas
2 tablespoons Vegenaise (or mayonnaise, or yogurt)
1 tablespoon nutritional yeast
Kosher salt
4 small (3 by 4 inches/7.5 by 10 cm) pieces snacking nori, plus more for serving

Prep the chickpeas: Drain and rinse 1 (14-ounce/400 g) can of chickpeas. Add to a bowl and crush well with a fork. Add 2 tablespoons of Vegenaise, 1 tablespoon nutritional yeast, a squeeze of lemon juice, and a good amount of salt. Crumble 4 sheets of nori and mix well to combine.

Prep the collard greens: Rinse the collard greens and pat dry with paper towels. Trim off the thick stem, and then use a little knife to shave the big rib down the middle of the leaf so it is smooth.

Prep the veggies: Slice 1 cucumber. Thinly slice ½ small red onion (60 g).

Assemble and serve: Put half of the chickpeas on each of the prepared collard green leaves. Top with sliced onion and cucumber and 1 cup (90 g) sprouts. Put additional nori on top, wrap up like a little burrito, and enjoy!

Mushroom "Carnitas" Tacos with Citrusy Radish Slaw

Makes 12 tacos

I am fascinated by the mushrooms at the farmers' markets, and big, furry lion's mane are one of the most intriguing varieties. These tacos are a perfect way to use them, because they have a meat-like texture and are little sponges for flavor. If you can't find them, try it with oyster, or sliced cremini (or you can even grow them at home—find kits from Smallhold and Northspore online!). Lion's mane has health benefits, including neuroregenerative properties, so it's a great 'shroom to work into your diet.

PRODUCE
2 oranges
1 pound (454 g) lion's mane mushrooms
½ head red cabbage
2 radishes
2 limes
1 bunch fresh cilantro
1 avocado

PANTRY
1 tablespoon vegetable or coconut oil
2 chipotles in adobo
1 tablespoon smoked soy sauce or 1 teaspoon
   smoked paprika
1 teaspoon garlic powder
Kosher salt and freshly ground black pepper
1 tablespoon mayonnaise
12 corn tortillas

Preheat the oven to 425°F (220°C).

Marinate the mushrooms: Juice 1½ oranges (to obtain about ½ cup/118 ml juice) into a large bowl. Add 1 tablespoon oil. Finely chop 2 chipotles in adobo and add them to the bowl. Whisk in 1 tablespoon smoked soy sauce, 1 teaspoon garlic powder, and season generously with salt and pepper. Pull apart 1 pound (454 g) lion's mane mushrooms into bite-size pieces and place them in the bowl. Toss them with the marinade until it is fully absorbed.

Cook the mushrooms: Spread the mushrooms onto a rimmed baking sheet. Bake until all the liquid is absorbed and the mushrooms are a deep golden brown and really crispy around the edges, 25 to 30 minutes.

Meanwhile, make the slaw: Using a mandoline, thinly shave ½ head red cabbage (the shavings should be about the thickness of two or three coins stacked together), add the shavings to a large bowl, and sprinkle with salt. Shave 2 radishes into the bowl. Squeeze the remaining ½ orange into the bowl, the juice from 1 lime, and 1 tablespoon mayonnaise. Remove the leaves from 1 bunch cilantro, give them a little chop, and toss everything together.

Char the tortillas: Using tongs, set 1 tortilla at a time directly over the flame of a gas burner or place in a cast-iron skillet over high heat. Cook until well charred in spots on both sides, about 1 minute per side. Wrap in a clean towel until ready to serve.

Assemble and serve: Slice the avocado.

Fill the tortillas with mushrooms and top with the slaw and sliced avocado. Serve with lime wedges.

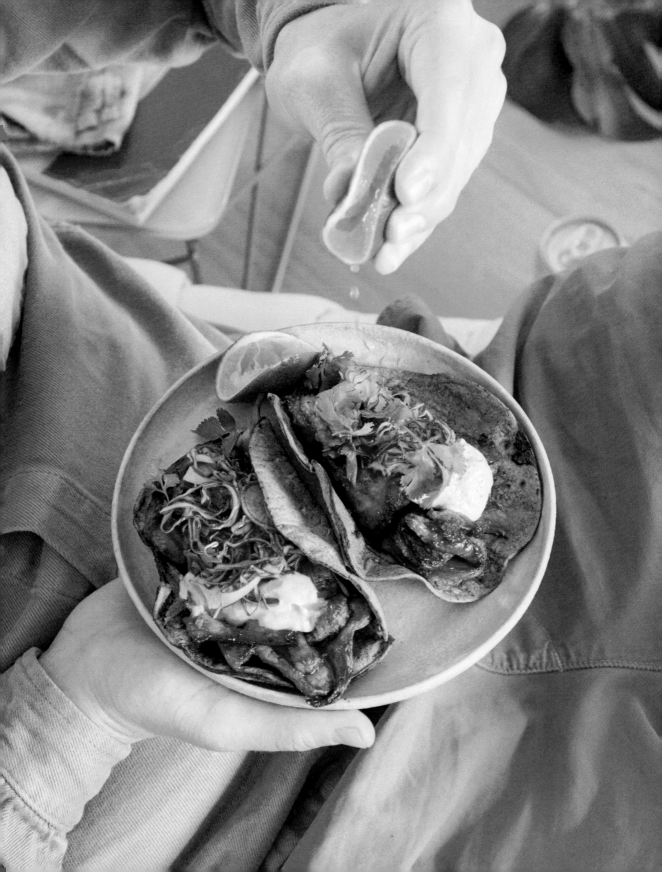

One-Pan Greek Lemon Chicken and Potatoes

Serves 4 to 6

Whenever I have a question about Greek food, I ask my friend Angelo. His mom, Maria, is always so sweet and sends a recipe right away. Angelo gave me this recipe for potatoes, which is perfect, but after discovering you could add a chicken to the same pan and make an entire meal, well, we now have this one on weekly rotation. The chicken drippings swirl with the bright tangy lemon and olive oil mixture coating the tender, sort-of half-crispy potatoes. Yes, there are a lot of recipes for roast chicken, but I think you'd be hard-pressed to find a more foolproof and flavorful dinner.

....

PRODUCE
1 pound (454 g) Yukon gold potatoes
2 heads garlic
2 lemons
3 sprigs fresh oregano

PROTEIN
1 (4½-pound/2 kg) chicken

PANTRY
Kosher salt and freshly ground black pepper
¼ cup (60 ml) extra-virgin olive oil
1 cup (240 ml) chicken stock, store-bought or
   homemade (page 265), or water

Prep the chicken: If you have the time, dry-brine the chicken up to 2 days or at least a couple of hours in advance: First, pat the chicken dry, then sprinkle inside and out with about 4 teaspoons salt, and then allow the chicken to sit in the fridge, uncovered, to dry out the skin as much as possible. If you don't have the time, at least season the chicken and allow it to come to room temperature before cooking.

When you're ready to make the chicken, preheat the oven to 350°F (175°C). Cut 2 heads garlic in half across the equator. Stick the garlic in the chicken cavity and tie up the legs if you have kitchen twine. Set on a rimmed, parchment-lined baking sheet.

Prep the veggies: Peel 1 pound (454 g) potatoes and cut them in half, and then in half again, into 2- to 3-inch (5 to 7.5 cm) Weeble Wobbles. Add the potatoes to the sheet pan along with ¼ cup (60 ml) olive oil, 1 cup (240 ml) chicken stock or water, the juice of 2 lemons, 3 sprigs oregano, and a generous amount of salt.

Cook until the potatoes are tender on the side touching the pan, but crispy on the outside, and the chicken reaches 160°F (70°C) when an instant-read thermometer is inserted in the thickest part of the thigh, about 1½ hours.

Carve and serve: Let the chicken rest 10 to 15 minutes before carving and serving with the potatoes.

DESSERTS & BAKED GOODS

The real magic of the night is when it all starts winding down. When you feel so at home you can unbutton your pants and pour yourself one more glass of chilled red. When you realize you are making full eye contact with the people around you and are asking them questions. The rest of the week has faded away, and honestly, the rest of the world, too. For me, this is quite literally the icing on the cake, when you've got everyone in the palm of your hand—people think it's all over, but you've got one more thing in the kitchen.

"Oh, I couldn't!"

"I'm so full!"

But you can. This is when the music slows down and the lights dim. We somehow always end up on the floor of the living room gathered around what used to be my low dining table in New York—why does dessert taste so much sweeter there? Put a warm cup of tea in everyone's hands and just a little something. Not too sweet, but full of flavors, sometimes familiar, but often something people just can't put their finger on. I think this is where a meal turns into something people dream about for days. Make people feel a little stoned, even if they aren't. Even just a single perfect bite to linger on during the car ride home.

For me, eating healthfully doesn't mean I never indulge. In fact, I eat a little date-sweetened dark chocolate just about every night. It does, however, mean that when I do bake, or make desserts, I use just enough natural sweetness to make the textures of the bake good work, and make the naturally sweet flavors of fruit, chocolate, and nuts really sing. Mostly because I think that is what tastes good.

Some of these desserts won't be for everyone. If you are used to super sugary sweets and processed ingredients, you may be disappointed—but I really don't think these recipes deprive you of anything. They have complex, fruity, nutty, and rich flavors and are naturally sweetened with dates, honey, and maple syrup whenever possible—real ingredients that add their own unique flavors as well as other nutrients. I find desserts like these to be really balanced—they absolutely satiate my sweet tooth without compromising what I'm looking for in a dessert in order to be overly healthy. They are still desserts, but I hope they can be eaten and shared and enjoyed without guilt or feeling like an unnecessary indulgence.

Sweet Potato Bread with Miso Tahini Butter

Makes one 9 by 5-inch (23 by 12 cm) loaf

Deb Perelman from Smitten Kitchen did a lot of research to find the perfect pumpkin bread recipe, and then one day, I changed it around a little bit and used sweet potatoes instead of pumpkin, and the rest is history. Sweet potatoes have an earthier flavor that I just love. Yes, there is regular sugar in this, but it's too perfect to alter any more than I did. Darren Romanelli promised he would make a limited-edition run of a tee-shirt for this bread, he loved it that much, so, if you're a fan . . . watch for that drop. *Do not skip* the miso tahini butter; in fact, you might want to make extra to have around for other breads.

PRODUCE
4 large orange-fleshed sweet potatoes

DAIRY
½ recipe Miso Tahini Butter (page 273)

PROTEIN
3 large eggs

PANTRY
½ cup (120 ml) vegetable or coconut oil
1 cup plus 2 tablespoons (225 g) cane sugar
2¼ cups (295 g) all-purpose flour
1½ teaspoons baking powder
¾ teaspoon baking soda
1 teaspoon kosher salt
¾ teaspoon plus 1 teaspoon ground cinnamon
¼ teaspoon fresh grated nutmeg
½ teaspoon ground ginger
Big pinch ground cloves

Bake the sweet potatoes: Preheat the oven to 425°F (220°C). Line a rimmed baking sheet with parchment paper, and place 4 sweet potatoes on it. Prick all over with a fork. Bake until tender, about 45 minutes. Let cool before removing the skins, then use a fork, potato masher, immersion blender, or food processor to create a smooth puree out of the flesh (about 1¾ cups/425 g).

Prep the pan: Preheat the oven to 350°F (175°C). Butter a 9 by 5-inch (23 by 12 cm) loaf pan.

Make the bread dough: In a large bowl, whisk together 1¾ cups (425 g) sweet potato puree, ½ cup (120 ml) vegetable oil, 3 large eggs, and 1 cup (200 g) cane sugar until smooth.

In another bowl, whisk together the 2¼ cups (295 g) flour, 1½ teaspoons baking powder, ¾ teaspoon baking soda, 1 teaspoon salt, ¾ teaspoon cinnamon, ¼ teaspoon nutmeg, ½ teaspoon ginger, and a big pinch of ground cloves until well combined. Add the dry ingredients to the wet and stir, just until combined. Scrape into the prepared pan and smooth the top.

Make the topping: In a small dish, stir 2 tablespoons cane sugar and 1 teaspoon cinnamon together. Sprinkle over the top of the batter.

Bake and serve: Bake the bread for 65 to 75 minutes, until a tester poked into all parts of the bread come out clean.

Let cool in the pan for 10 minutes and then remove the loaf, or let it cool completely in the pan before serving with miso tahi butter. I don't think you'll have any leftovers, but if you do, wrap in foil or plastic wrap and enjoy for up to 4 days.

Date-Sweetened Carrot Cake

Serves 8 to 12

This recipe calls for a lot of dates, like maybe what seems like an unreasonable amount of dates—but it's an extremely rich cake and, I think, absolutely worth it. It feels so moist, sweet, and decadent. The frosting is also sweetened with dates, which makes it taste more brown buttery and caramelly than a simple cream cheese frosting. Easily make the cake vegan by swapping eggs for flaxseed eggs and use your favorite vegan cream cheese and vegan butter for the frosting. I love the frosting to be kind of tart and not too sweet, but add another ½ cup (95 g) of dates or a bit of maple syrup if you prefer it on the sweeter side.

PRODUCE
1 pound (454 g) carrots

DAIRY
2 (8-ounce/226 g) blocks or containers cream cheese or vegan cream cheese, at room temperature
½ cup (1 stick/113 g) unsalted butter or vegan butter, at room temperature

PROTEIN
4 large eggs

PANTRY
2½ cups (315 g) all-purpose flour, plus more for the pans
2 teaspoons baking soda
1 tablespoon ground cinnamon
2 teaspoons ground ginger
¼ teaspoon freshly ground nutmeg
½ teaspoon kosher salt, plus more for the frosting
1 cup (240 ml) coconut oil, plus more for the pan
4½ cups/about 27 ounces (766 g) pitted, dried Medjool dates
1½ cups (360 ml) hot water
2 teaspoons vanilla extract
1½ cups (180 g) walnuts, toasted (see page 33) and crushed
1 (8-ounce/227 g) can crushed pineapple in juice (no sugar added)

Make the cake batter: Preheat the oven to 350ºF (175ºC).

In a medium bowl, combine 2½ cups (315 g) flour, 2 teaspoons baking soda, 1 tablespoon cinnamon, 2 teaspoons ginger, ¼ teaspoon nutmeg, and ½ teaspoon salt. Use a bit of coconut oil to grease two 9-inch (23 cm) round cake pans. Add a circle of parchment paper to each, oil the paper with more coconut oil, and then sprinkle with a bit of flour, tapping it around in the pan a bit to coat all sides. Tap out any excess flour and discard.

You'll need to use a food processor to puree the dates, so first I would recommend using the grating attachment to grate 1 pound (454 g) carrots to yield 3 cups and set them aside. Wipe out the processor and add 3 cups (517 g) of the dates and 1½ cups (360 ml) very hot water. Let the dates soak for at least 5 minutes to soften and to allow the water to cool down a bit. Carefully pulse until smooth.

Add 1 cup (240 ml) coconut oil to the food processor and continue to pulse until blended. Add 1 teaspoon of the vanilla, then 4 eggs, one at a time, and pulse until combined, scraping down the sides as needed.

Transfer the wet mixture to the bowl with the dry

(Continued)

ingredients and fold to combine. Stir in 1½ cups (180 g) crushed walnuts, 1 (8-ounce/227 g) can crushed pineapple, and the reserved carrots. Mix the batter just until smooth.

Bake the cake: Divide the batter evenly between the two prepared pans and bake until a toothpick inserted into the center of the cake comes out clean, 35 to 40 minutes. Cool in the pans for about 10 minutes, before turning out on a cooling rack to cool completely.

Meanwhile, make the frosting: Wipe out the food processor and add the remaining 1½ cups (249 g) pitted dates to the bowl (or 2 cups if you already know you like things a little sweeter—you can always add a bit of maple syrup later). Add ½ cup (120 ml) hot water and let sit for 5 minutes. Blend until smooth and let cool completely. Add 1 pound (452 g) room-temperature cream cheese or vegan cream cheese. Add ½ cup (1 stick/113 g) room-temperature unsalted butter or vegan butter. Add the remaining 1 teaspoon vanilla and season with 1 generous pinch salt. Blend until smooth. Taste for sweetness, and add a bit of maple syrup if desired.

Assemble the cake: Use a sharp, serrated knife to trim the tops of the two cake layers. Place one cake cut side up on a serving platter and spread with about 1½ cups (370 g) frosting. Place the second cake layer cut side down on top of the first.

Use the remaining frosting to coat the top and sides of the cake. Cover with plastic wrap and store in the refrigerator for up to 4 days. Bring the cake to room temperature before serving.

Buckwheat Brownies

Makes 16

When I was a child, we used to go to Key West almost every winter. I was small, and I don't remember much, except for the call of a woman on a bicycle who, year after year, would yell out "warm and chewy" while selling fat brownies from her basket around Mallory Square. The truth is I can't remember if I ever even had one, but the call will ring in my head forever. These brownies are only sweetened with plump juicy dates, so they are incredibly chewy with a complex flavor, and fabulous right out of the oven when they are warm. There is caramel and nuttiness and rich dark chocolate. And! They are gluten-free.

....

DAIRY
½ cup (1 stick/113 g) unsalted butter, cut into pieces, plus more for the pan

PROTEIN
3 large eggs

PANTRY
12 ounces (340 g) pitted, dried Medjool dates (about 20)
½ cup (120 ml) hot water
6 ounces (170 g) unsweetened chocolate chips
¼ cup (25 g) unsweetened cocoa powder
½ teaspoon kosher salt
¾ cup (90 g) buckwheat flour
Flaky salt

Prep the pan: Preheat the oven to 350ºF (175ºC). Brush an 8-inch (20 cm) square baking pan with butter, and line it with parchment paper, leaving an overhang on two sides. Butter the parchment.

Make the batter: Add 12 ounces (340 g) dates to the bowl of a food processor and carefully pour ½ cup (120 ml) hot water on top. Let the dates soak for at least 10 minutes while you prepare the chocolate.

In a heat-safe bowl, either melt ½ cup (1 stick/113 g) butter and 6 ounces (170 g) chocolate chips by setting the bowl over a saucepan with a couple of inches of simmering water or by heating them in 30-second intervals in the microwave. Stir frequently.

Process the dates and hot water until completely smooth—this will take a few minutes. Then add the chocolate and butter mixture. Process until smooth. Add 3 eggs, one at a time, and process until completely combined. Scrape down the sides as needed. Add ¼ cup (25 g) cocoa powder, ½ teaspoon salt, and ¾ cup (90 g) buckwheat flour and pulse until everything is combined. It may need a good fold with a rubber spatula before you transfer it to the prepared pan and sprinkle with flaky salt.

Bake and serve: Bake until a toothpick inserted in the center comes out clean, 30 to 35 minutes. Let cool almost completely in the pan. Lift the brownies out of the pan using the parchment paper overhang and cut into 16 squares. Store in an airtight container for up to 4 days.

Cookies and Treats

Dad's World-Famous Oatmeal Raisin Cookies

Makes 22

My dad has declared many of his recipes "world famous," including the clam chowder that he has only, in my memory, made a single time. But these cookies are on regular rotation and are asked for and remembered by many. Sometimes there are walnuts in them, and sometimes they sit a little taller or have little chunks of granola in them, if that's what's in the pantry. My parents never had proper measuring cups or spoons in the kitchen, so these cookies have been a little different every time he's made them. He would send big bags of them up to college often, so I know they store and ship well, and to me, they taste just like home.

DAIRY
¾ cup (1½ sticks /170 g) unsalted butter, at room temperature

PROTEIN
3 large egg yolks

PANTRY
1¼ cups (155 g) all-purpose flour
½ cup (60 g) wheat germ
1 teaspoon baking soda
2 teaspoons ground cinnamon
Pinch freshly ground nutmeg
1 teaspoon kosher salt
¾ cup (180 ml) pure maple syrup
2 teaspoons vanilla extract
3 cups (340 g) old-fashioned (not thick-cut) oats
1 cup (166 g) raisins

Preheat the oven to 350°F (175°C). Line two baking sheets with parchment paper.

Mix the dry ingredients: In a medium bowl, combine 1¼ cups (155 g) all-purpose flour, ½ cup (60 g) wheat germ, 1 teaspoon baking soda, 2 teaspoons cinnamon, 1 pinch nutmeg, and 1 teaspoon salt and whisk together.

Make the dough: In the bowl of an electric stand mixer fitted with the paddle attachment, beat ¾ cup (1½ sticks/170 g) butter until it's soft and fluffy, 3 to 4 minutes. In a slow steady stream, start adding ¾ cup (180 ml) maple syrup, stopping to scrape down the sides as necessary. Keep beating until the mixture is light and fluffy, about 6 minutes. Add 3 egg yolks, one at a time, beating and scraping down the sides after each addition. If the dough starts to look a little broken, just let it mix for a few more minutes until everything looks pretty creamy and smooth. Mix in 2 teaspoons vanilla.

With the mixer on low speed, beat in the flour mixture until just combined and scrape down the sides of the bowl. Add 3 cups (340 g) oats and mix until just combined, then add 1 cup (166 g) raisins. Give the dough a good stir by hand to make sure the raisins are mixed into the batter evenly.

Bake the cookies: Use a 2-ounce (60 ml) ice cream scoop to portion the dough on the prepared baking sheets. I fit 12 cookies per tray. Bake, rotating the pans once, until the cookies are deep golden brown on the sides and bottoms, 18 to 20 minutes. Allow the cookies to cool completely on the pans. They are very delicate when they first come out of the oven. Enjoy when they're cool or store in an airtight container at room temperature for up to 4 days or freeze unbaked dough for up to 3 months.

Chocolate-Covered Stuffed Dates

Makes 10

If you can't tell already, I really love dates. This is a super simple treat to have ready in the freezer for guests, or just to pop a couple on a plate when you're watching TV at night with a cup of tea. Feel free to switch out the tahini for peanut butter or almond butter and top with crushed peanuts or almonds!

PANTRY
10 pitted, dried Medjool dates
2 tablespoons tahini
½ cup (70 g) chopped unsweetened or date-
    sweetened dark chocolate
2 teaspoons coconut oil
2 tablespoons pistachios, finely chopped
Flaky salt

Prep the dates: Slice a small slit lengthwise into each date, being careful not to cut them in half. Spoon a little tahini in each slit, then arrange the dates on a small plate or baking sheet that can fit in the freezer. Freeze while you melt the chocolate.

Melt the chocolate: Combine ½ cup (70 g) chocolate and 2 teaspoons coconut oil in a heat-safe bowl. Microwave in 30-second intervals until melted and smooth.

Assemble and freeze: Dip the frozen dates in the melted chocolate and sprinkle with 2 tablespoons pistachios and flaky salt. Return to the freezer to set, then transfer to an airtight container and return to the freezer for up to 2 months or until you get the urge for a little something sweet.

Salty Honey Peanut Butter Cookies

Makes 12 cookies

Ovenly, the Brooklyn bakery, created the ultimate gluten-free peanut butter cookie recipe that comes together in minutes, and this is my ode to that cookie—but mine is sweetened with honey to bring in that honey-roasted peanut flavor in a never-ending attempt to satisfy Ben's craving for Peanut Lover's Chex Mix (RIP).

PROTEIN
2 large eggs

PANTRY
1¼ cups (300 ml) honey
1 teaspoon vanilla extract
1¾ cups (415 ml) unsweetened smooth peanut
    butter
Flaky salt

Preheat the oven to 350°F (175°C) and line a rimmed baking sheet with parchment paper.

Make the cookie dough: In a large bowl, whisk together 1¼ cups (300 ml) honey, 2 eggs, and 1 teaspoon vanilla until smooth. Fold in 1¾ cups (415 ml) peanut butter with a spatula until fully combined.

Assemble and bake: Use a 2-ounce (60 ml) ice cream scoop to form twelve 2-inch (2.5 cm) cookies. Sprinkle the cookies with flaky salt. Bake on the upper rack of the oven until lightly golden and cracked on top, 20 to 25 minutes. The cookies will be very fragile, so let them cool completely before serving! Store in an airtight container for up to 3 days.

Hazelnut and Carob Thumbprints

Makes about 24 cookies

I didn't think I could write a book on health food without including carob. A lot of people who grew up in the seventies and eighties seem to be traumatized by the ingredient, but that's because it was passed off as a chocolate substitute. There is no substitute for chocolate, and you can't go into this cookie expecting it to be chocolate—you have to just appreciate the carob for what it is—a nutty, delicious substance, with its own unique flavor. Brad Leone, my longtime friend and a YouTube star, has been championing carob since at least 2010; I hope to join him in the movement with this recipe. Also, this is a naturally gluten-free cookie!

DAIRY
½ cup (1 stick/113 g) unsalted butter, at room temperature
2 large egg yolks

PANTRY
¼ cup (60 ml) coconut cream
¼ cup (60 g) carob powder
½ cup (90 g) coconut sugar
1 teaspoon cornstarch
2 cups (200 g) hazelnut flour
Pinch ground cinnamon
¼ teaspoon kosher salt
Pinch flaky salt

Make the "ganache": In a small bowl, combine ¼ cup (60 ml) coconut cream and ¼ cup (60 g) carob powder. Whisk until smooth. Set aside.

Make the cookie dough: Preheat the oven to 350ºF (175ºF). Line two baking sheets with parchment paper.

In a food processor, combine ½ cup (90 g) coconut sugar and 1 teaspoon cornstarch until powdered. Add ½ cup (1 stick/113 g) butter and blend until combined, scraping down the sides as needed. Add 2 egg yolks and mix until combined, about 1 minute. Add 2 cups (200 g) hazelnut flour, 1 pinch cinnamon, and ¼ teaspoon salt. Mix until just combined. Chill the dough for at least 20 minutes before scooping.

Assemble and bake: Using 1 tablespoon dough for each cookie, roll the dough into balls and place them onto the prepared baking sheets, spacing the cookies about 1 inch (2.5 cm) apart. Make an indentation in the center of each ball with a small measuring spoon or the handle end of a wooden spoon.

Bake until the cookies are set and golden around the edges, 16 to 18 minutes, rotating the baking sheets halfway through. Transfer the baking sheets to wire racks and let cool for 5 minutes, then transfer the cookies to the racks and let them cool completely. Add a teaspoon of ganache to each cookie, and swirl a bit with a spoon, or flatten/smooth with an offset spatula. Store in an airtight container for up to 4 days.

Oat Bars with Rhubarb Ginger Jam

Makes 16

I made these bars once years ago, and Lauryn and Shira (who both worked at Martha and are amazing cooks) are still talking about them, so they had to be included here. I make this quick, low-sugar jam because I prefer it over the super-sweet store-bought options. Lauryn also told me once that rhubarb smells like God, so I'm hoping that somehow makes up for the fact that these are not fully health food.

PRODUCE

1 pound (454 g) rhubarb (about 2 stalks)
1 pint (400 g) fresh strawberries
2-inch (5 cm) piece fresh ginger
Juice of ½ lemon

PANTRY

1 cup (180 g) plus ⅔ cup (60 g) coconut sugar
1¼ cups (140 g) old-fashioned oats
1 teaspoon cornstarch or tapioca or potato starch
1¼ cups (156 g) all-purpose (or gluten-free 1 to 1 all-purpose) flour
1 teaspoon kosher salt
1 vanilla bean
Kosher salt
½ teaspoon ground cinnamon

DAIRY

1 cup (2 sticks/226 g) cold unsalted butter, or vegan butter, plus more for the pan

Make the jam: Chop 1 pound (454 g) rhubarb stalks into ¼-inch-thick (6 mm) pieces. Hull and thinly slice 1 pint (400 g) strawberries. Peel 2 inches (5 cm) ginger and grate using a Microplane. Combine the rhubarb, 1 cup (180 g) of the coconut sugar, and ginger in a medium pot. Bring to a boil and cook until the rhubarb is softened, about 10 minutes, then reduce the heat to a rapid simmer. Cook until the jam thickens and the rhubarb dissolves, about 30 minutes. Let cool for at least 30 minutes before assembling and baking the bars.

Meanwhile, make the crust: Preheat the oven to 325°F (165°C). Add 1¼ cups (140 g) oats to a rimmed baking sheet and toast until lightly brown, about 5 minutes. Cut 1 cup (2 sticks/226 g) cold butter into pieces.

In a food processor, combine the remaining ⅔ cup (60 g) coconut sugar and 1 teaspoon cornstarch and process until powdered. Add 1 cup (80 g) toasted oats and pulse until finely ground. Add the butter and process until the mixture is crumbly but holds together.

Butter the bottom of an 8-inch (20 cm) square baking pan, line with parchment paper, and butter again. Transfer half the dough to the pan and press firmly into the bottom with a measuring cup. Use a fork to make a couple of prick marks around the dough square. Bake until lightly browned, about 25 minutes, and let the crust cool slightly, about 10 minutes.

Assemble and bake: Bring the oven back up to 325°F (165°C). Spread the jam (you should have about 1½ cups/355 ml) over the cooled crust.

In a small bowl, combine the remaining ¼ cup (40 g) toasted oats and ½ teaspoon cinnamon. Scatter the topping over the bars, squeezing some of the mixture together to create clumps.

Bake until the topping becomes light brown, about 20 minutes. Transfer to a rack to cool completely, before cutting into squares and serving. Store in an airtight container for up to 3 days.

Health Nut

Sesame Spelt Banana Bread

Makes one 9 by 5-inch (23 by 13 cm) loaf

Not too sweet, and very roasty, toasty, and caramelized—this is the banana bread of my dreams. Spelt has an extremely nutty flavor but still allows for a beautiful texture in baked goods. Using frozen and thawed bananas and incorporating their juices may seem annoying, but it's worth it—the banana liquid is SO flavorful and concentrated. My friend Greg Lofts taught me this method and I never turned back! Also, if you like a chocolate chip in your banana bread, stir in 1 cup (175 g) dark chocolate chips or chunks into the batter before pouring into the prepared pan!

....

PRODUCE
4 very ripe medium bananas, frozen and thawed

PROTEIN
3 large eggs

PANTRY
⅓ cup (90 ml) extra-virgin olive oil, plus more for the pan
¾ cup (130 g) plus 1 tablespoon packed brown sugar
2 tablespoons tahini
2 teaspoons vanilla extract
1¾ cup (290 g) spelt flour
½ cup (70 g) toasted black sesame seeds
1 teaspoon baking soda
½ teaspoon kosher salt

Prep the pan: Preheat the oven to 350°F (175°C). Brush a 9 by 5-inch (23 by 13 cm) loaf pan with a bit of olive oil and line with parchment paper, leaving an overhang on two sides.

Prep the banana mixture: Add the 4 thawed bananas and their juices to a medium bowl. Smash well with a fork until it's almost a puree (a few lumps are okay!). Add ¾ cup (130 g) brown sugar, 3 large eggs, ⅓ cup (60 ml) oil, 2 tablespoons tahini, and 2 teaspoons vanilla and whisk until combined.

Mix the bread: In a large bowl, combine 1¾ cups (290 g) spelt flour, ¼ cup (35 g) sesame seeds, 1 teaspoon baking soda, and ½ teaspoon salt. Add the banana mixture to the bowl and fold to combine.

Bake the bread: Pour the batter into the prepared load pan. Sprinkle with the remaining 1 tablespoon brown sugar and the remaining ¼ cup (35 g) sesame seeds. Bake until golden brown and a toothpick or knife inserted in the center of the loaf comes out with a few moist crumbs attached, 50 to 60 minutes. Let the bread cool slightly before serving.

Keeps in the fridge, wrapped in plastic wrap, for about 4 days.

Simple Any-Stone-Fruit Cake

Serves 8 to 10

In 1983, Marian Burros made the perfect cake recipe for a plum torte, and essentially no one has needed to make a cake recipe again. I tweaked the recipe, and included it in this book, because I want everyone to understand the versatility of this cake and celebrate it by making it all the time. Instead of plums, add peaches, apricots, pluots, apples, pears, or maybe even cherries with some chocolate. It comes together in minutes, and you can truly use what you have on hand and have a dessert to wrap up any dinner party.

....

PRODUCE
8 plums, peaches, pluots, cherries, or apricots
1 lemon

PROTEIN
2 large eggs

DAIRY
½ cup (1 stick/113 g) unsalted butter, at room temperature

PANTRY
1 cup (125 g) all-purpose (or gluten-free 1 to 1 all-purpose) flour
1 teaspoon baking powder
¼ teaspoon kosher salt
¾ cup (150 g) cane sugar, plus a little more for sprinkling
2 teaspoons vanilla extract or paste
Sprinkle ground cinnamon

Prep the pan and the fruit: Preheat the oven to 350ºF (175ºC). Butter a 10-inch (25 cm) cast-iron skillet or deep-dish pie plate. Remove the pits from 8 plums or fruit of choice, and cut into ¾-inch (2 cm) wedges, or halve the cherries.

Make the batter: In a medium bowl, whisk together 1 cup (125 g) flour, 1 teaspoon baking powder, and ¼ teaspoon salt.

In the bowl of an electric mixer, combine ¾ cup (150 g) sugar and ½ cup (1 stick/113 g) butter and the zest of 1 lemon and beat until light and fluffy, scraping down the sides as needed, about 6 minutes.

Add the vanilla and beat to combine. Add 2 eggs, one at a time, and beat, scraping down the sides of the bowl until a paste-like batter forms.

Assemble and bake the cake: Transfer the batter into the prepared pan and smooth the top (it will be quite thick). Add the fruit, cut side down, to the cake in a sort of circular pattern. Sprinkle it with a little sugar, cinnamon, and a little squeeze of lemon.

Bake until a toothpick inserted in the center comes out clean, 20 to 25 minutes. I can never wait until the cake cools even slightly and tend to serve it minutes after it comes out of the oven while it still has a custardy texture.

Almond Shortcake with Peaches

Makes 6

Shortcakes are the perfect summertime treat. Any time I've brought them out at a party people have been so excited. I love the zing of tart raspberries and ginger to balance out the sweetness of juicy peaches, but feel free to swap in any other peak-season fruit.

....

PRODUCE
4 peaches
2 pints (340 g) fresh raspberries
½ lemon
1-inch (2.5 cm) piece fresh ginger

DAIRY
¼ cup (½ stick/55 g) cold unsalted butter
½ cup plus 1 tablespoon (250 ml) unsweetened plain or coconut yogurt, plus more for serving

PANTRY
1¼ cups (155 g) all-purpose (or gluten-free 1 to 1 all-purpose) flour
½ cup (60 g) almond flour
1 tablespoon baking powder
½ teaspoon baking soda
½ teaspoon kosher salt
5 tablespoons (63 g) coconut sugar, plus more for sprinkling and topping (optional)
½ teaspoon almond extract
1 vanilla bean or 2 teaspoons vanilla extract

Preheat the oven to 350ºF (175ºC). Line a baking sheet with parchment paper.

Make the shortcakes: In a food processor, combine 1¼ cups (155 g) all-purpose flour, ½ cup (60 g) almond flour, 1 tablespoon baking powder, ½ teaspoon baking soda, ½ teaspoon salt, and 3 tablespoons coconut sugar. Pulse to combine. Add ¼ cup (½ stick/55 g) cold butter, chopped into pieces, and pulse exactly 12 times. Add ½ teaspoon almond extract and ½ cup (120 ml)

yogurt, and pulse just until the dough comes together. Place the dough on a clean work surface and gently flatten it out without handling it too much—just to work in any dry bits and make a rough 5 by 6-inch (12.5 by 15 cm) rectangle—and fold it on top of itself. Do this once more. Cut into 6 pieces or use a 2-ounce (60 ml) scoop to portion out rustic little biscuits.

Transfer the cakes to the prepared baking sheet, and if you can find room in your freezer, chill for 10 minutes. Brush the tops with the remaining 1 tablespoon Greek yogurt thinned with 1 tablespoon of water, sprinkle with a little sugar, and bake until beautifully puffed and deep golden brown, about 25 minutes.

Meanwhile, make the filling: Thinly slice 4 peaches and add to a large bowl with 2 pints (340 g) raspberries, 2 tablespoons sugar, and the zest and juice of ½ lemon. Scrape ½ vanilla bean into the bowl, or add 1 teaspoon vanilla extract. Peel and mince 1 inch (2.5 cm) ginger and add. Toss it and let the filling macerate in the fridge for at least 20 minutes, up to 3 hours.

Add a bit of yogurt to a small bowl. Scrape the seeds from the remaining ½ vanilla bean into the bowl, or add the remaining 1 teaspoon vanilla extract. Stir to combine. Sweeten just a bit with coconut sugar if desired. Whip until soft peaks form, about 2 minutes.

Assemble and serve: Cut the shortcakes in half and fill each one with a generous amount of fruit and a dollop of the topping. These biscuits can be eaten the next day if stored in an airtight container, but are really best enjoyed the same day they are made.

Vegan Baklava Ice Cream

Makes about 1 quart (950 ml)

Baklava is one of my all-time favorite desserts. While this vegan ice cream doesn't have any flaky phyllo dough, I love being able to experience the flavor profile I love so much in a completely different way. Coconut cream makes a dreamy base that is so rich you really won't believe it's not custard.

....

PRODUCE
1 lemon

PANTRY
2 (14-ounce/400 g) cans coconut cream
½ cup (120 ml) honey
1 teaspoon ground cinnamon
1 tablespoon vanilla paste
Pinch kosher salt
¼ cup (60 ml) pistachio butter (see Nut Butter, page 266)
¼ cup (30 g) crushed toasted pistachios
¼ cup (30 g) crushed toasted walnuts (see page 33)
Dried food-grade rose petals

Make the ice cream: In a medium bowl, whisk together two 14-ounce (400 g) cans coconut cream, ½ cup (120 ml) honey, 1 teaspoon cinnamon, 1 tablespoon vanilla paste, zest of 1 lemon, and 1 pinch salt. Transfer the mixture to your ice cream maker and freeze according to the machine's instructions.

Add the swirl and toppings: Once frozen, use a silicone spatula to fold in ¼ cup (60 ml) pistachio butter. Transfer to a 9 by 5-inch (23 by 12 cm) baking dish or a plastic quart (liter) container with a lid, top with the crushed nuts and dried rose petals, and return to the freezer for up to 3 weeks or until ready to serve.

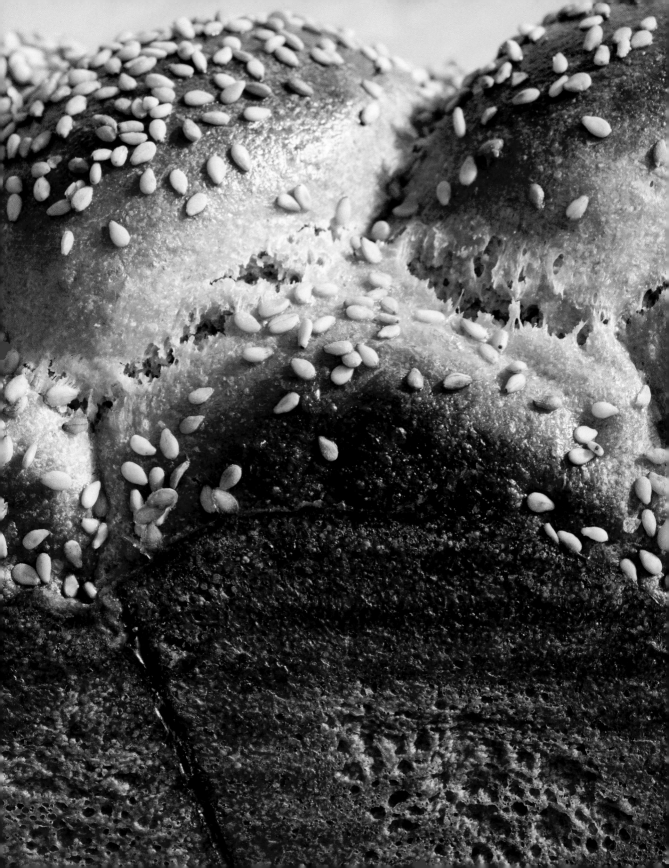

Whole-Wheat Sesame Challah

Makes two 9 by 5-inch (23 by 15 cm) loaves

If you've never baked bread in your life, I think this is a very rewarding place to start. There are no sourdough starters, and challah requires less patience than most bread. The most difficult part is braiding it, but luckily, there is YouTube for guidance, if my words fail you. The flavor that whole wheat gives this challah is incredible. Use it for the French toast on page 42, but also just enjoy it in your life.

....

PROTEIN
4 large eggs plus 1 egg for egg wash

PANTRY
3¾ teaspoons (14 g) active dry yeast (2 packages)
½ cup (120 ml) plus 1 tablespoon local honey
1¾ cups (414 ml) lukewarm water
½ cup (120 ml) really good-quality, fruity extra-virgin olive oil, plus some for greasing bowl
1 tablespoon kosher salt
8 cups (1040 g) whole-wheat flour
Sesame seeds, for finishing
Flaky salt, for finishing

Mix the dough: In a large bowl, or the bowl of an electric stand mixer (it has to be the big one!), dissolve 3¾ teaspoons (14 g) yeast and 1 tablespoon honey in the 1¾ cups warm water; set aside for about 5 minutes, or until it starts to get foamy.

Whisk ½ cup (120 ml) oil into the yeast, then beat in 4 large eggs, one at a time, with ½ cup (120 ml) honey and 1 tablespoon kosher salt. Gradually add 8 cups (1040 g) flour, 1 cup at a time. When the dough starts coming together, turn out onto a flour-coated surface to knead by hand, or use the dough hook attachment on your mixer (it really strains the machine, but it can technically do it). Knead until the dough is nice and smooth, like a little baby, as my friend Sam would say.

Clean out whatever big bowl you made the dough in, grease it with a little oil and return the dough to the clean bowl. Cover it with plastic wrap and let the dough rise in a warm place for 1 hour, until almost doubled in size (or put it in the fridge overnight and continue in the morning if you want flavors to further develop—if you do this, bring it to room temperature before proceeding). Punch down the dough, cover, and let it rise again in a warm place for another 30 minutes.

Divide the dough in half. You can do this with a scale, but I never do: take half the dough and form it into 6 equalish balls. Roll each ball into a foot-long (30 cm) strand. Place the 6 strands in a row, parallel to one another. Pinch the tops of the strands together. Move the outside right strand over 2 strands. Then take the second strand from the left and move it to the far right. Take the outside left strand and move it over one. Move the second strand from the right over to the far left. Start over with the outside right strand. Repeat until all strands are braided. Tuck the ends underneath. Repeat with the other half of the dough. Place the braided loaves in two 9 by 5-inch (23 by 15 cm) baking pans.

Beat the remaining 1 egg and brush the loaves. Cover with a towel. Let the dough rise for about another hour.

Bake the bread: Preheat the oven to 375°F (190°C) and brush the loaves with egg wash again. Sprinkle the loaves with a generous amount of sesame seeds and some flaky salt and bake in the middle of the oven for 30 to 40 minutes, or until golden. (If you have an instant-read thermometer, you can take it out when the bread hits an internal temperature of 190°F/90°C.) Cool the loaves on a rack. Tightly wrap in plastic wrap to store.

Masa Harina Cornbread

Makes one 10-inch (25 cm) round bread

I started baking with good-quality masa instead of cornmeal last year when I wanted cornbread but was out of cornmeal. Now I'm never turning back! The masa gives cornbread such incredible flavor, aroma, and a different melt-in-your-mouth texture that I love. It's also pretty great with the Miso Tahini Butter (page 273), and perfect with the chili on page 103.

....

DAIRY
½ cup (1 stick/113 g) unsalted butter, or vegan butter, plus more for serving
1½ cups (360 ml) milk, or nut milk, store-bought or homemade (page 266)

PROTEIN
2 large eggs

PANTRY
1½ cups (200 g) masa harina
½ cup (76 g) whole-wheat flour
1 tablespoon baking powder
1 teaspoon kosher salt
¼ cup (60 ml) honey, plus more for serving
Flaky salt, for finishing

Preheat the oven to 425°F (225°C).

Prep the batter: Add ½ cup (1 stick/113 g) butter to a 10-inch (25 cm) cast-iron skillet and transfer it to the oven, just to melt, 3 to 5 minutes.

Meanwhile, in a large bowl, whisk together 1½ cups (200 g) masa harina, ½ cup (76 g) flour, 1 tablespoon baking powder, and 1 teaspoon salt.

Carefully transfer all but about 2 tablespoons of the melted butter into another large heatproof bowl. Add ¼ cup (60 ml) honey and whisk until melted and fully combined. Mix in 1½ cups (360 ml) milk. When cool to the touch, add 2 eggs and whisk everything until well combined.

Pour the wet batter into the dry ingredients and mix to combine.

Bake the bread: Swirl the remaining 2 tablespoons melted butter around in the skillet to make sure the sides are coated. Transfer the batter into the pan and smooth the top. Bake until golden brown and fragrant, 18 to 20 minutes.

Serve: Serve warm with more butter and honey and a good sprinkle of flaky salt. Store in an airtight container for up to 2 days; reheat in a 350°F (175°C) oven or pop in the microwave before serving.

STAPLES, DRESSINGS & SAUCES

● Staples

These are things I that I like to keep prepped all the time, because they make it easier to put together healthy, flavorful meals faster. You can buy all these foods, but you'll be amazed how easy (and affordable) they are to make at home.

....

Basic Breadcrumbs

Makes 4 cups (226 g)

Use up your stale bread, and always have the best-tasting breadcrumbs on hand.

8 ounces (225 g) sourdough or other white bread

Preheat the oven to 350°F (175°C). Tear 8 ounces (225 g) bread apart with your hands a little bit before adding to a food processor. Pulse until the bread forms fine-ish crumbs. Transfer to a rimmed baking sheet. Bake until the crumbs are dry and golden brown, 10 to 15 minutes, stirring a few times. Keep in an airtight container for up to 1 month.

Chicken or Veg Stock

Makes 4 quarts (about 4 liters)

Store-bought broths and stocks have lots of salt. This recipe has none, so keep that in mind when seasoning meals that use it. (Try a fun experiment: Taste one spoonful of your stock and then add a couple grains of salt to another spoonful. Taste the difference? Salt brings the flavor to life.) If you want to make a vegetarian stock, omit the chicken, obviously. Add 8 ounces (225 g) mushrooms, and maybe a leek, a couple of tablespoons of tomato paste or a sheet of kombu.

1 chicken (about 4 pounds/1.8 g), or same weight of chicken wings
1 large yellow onion, halved

1 head garlic, halved
2 carrots, halved
2 stalks celery, halved
½ bunch fresh parsley
2 bay leaves
1 teaspoon black peppercorns

Place all the ingredients in a very large pot (a stockpot if you own one) and add enough cold water to cover. I add 5 quarts (4.7 liters). Bring to a boil, then reduce to a gentle simmer. Cook for about 3 hours, occasionally skimming the foam off the top with a spoon. Strain the stock through a fine-mesh sieve into a large bowl and discard the solids (or eat the carrots and celery, like I do). To store, cool and refrigerate in a sealed container for a few days, or freeze for a couple of months.

Crispy Leeks

Makes about 3 cups

Mild and sweet leeks add big flavor and texture to everything when they are sizzled!

4 large leeks
½ inch (1.25 cm) avocado oil
Kosher salt

Cut off the white and light green parts from 4 large leeks (you can discard the dark green parts or save them for stock), thinly slice, and clean and spin them dry in a salad spinner. Heat ½ inch (1.25 cm) avocado oil in a cast-iron skillet over medium heat until shimmering.

Add half of the thinly sliced whites from the leeks and cook until golden brown and crispy, about 15 minutes. Remove and set on a paper towel–lined plate to drain. Sprinkle them with a bit of salt. Store in an airtight container at room temperature for up to 5 days.

Grow-Your-Own Sprouts

This is extremely simple to do, and it's so great to have a variety of fresh sprouts on hand all the time so you can add them to EVERYTHING. The easiest way to grow them is using a seed-sprouting kit that includes two glass jars with mesh lids, and a stand that will keep them inverted and catch any water. Organic seeds are available in bulk online. Broccoli sprouts are a really good place to start, but there are alfalfa seeds, mung beans, lentils, flavorful radish onion, and fenugreek . . . a whole new world is about to open up for you!

2 teaspoons organic sprouting seeds, such as broccoli or alfalfa

Place about 1 teaspoon sprouting seeds in each jar.

Soak in at least 2 inches (5 cm) filtered water in a dark place for 6 to 8 hours, then drain completely.

Rinse and strain the sprouting seeds twice a day, setting the jars in the tray stands to collect any excess water. The sprouts will start to grow in 3 to 5 days! Once the leaves are yellow, move the sprouts into a bit more sun to turn green. Store the sprouts in a produce bag or in the jar in the fridge for up to 3 days.

Nut Butter

Makes 1½ cups (355 ml)

Pistachio is a favorite, but pecan or almond with a little bit of maple syrup is pretty amazing, too. This is a really fun place to get creative and make up your own favorites. I love doing a mix of nuts and stirring some seeds in at the end to make an everything crunchy butter.

3 cups (375 g) raw pistachios or your preferred nut or a combination
Kosher salt
2 to 4 tablespoons maple syrup, agave, or your preferred sweetener (optional)

Preheat the oven to 400°F (205°C). Spread out 3 cups (375 g) nuts on a rimmed baking sheet and toast in the oven. Be careful not to burn them—set a timer, starting at 8 minutes, but keep checking as soon as they are slightly browned and fragrant. It shouldn't take more than 10 minutes, depending on what nuts you are using.

Add the toasted nuts to a food processor and process until smooth. This will be very loud, and it will take longer than you think, about 10 minutes. Scrape down the sides as needed and add about ½ teaspoon salt and taste for seasoning. Add sweetener of choice, if using, plus any other mix-ins to taste. I like to store mine in the fridge, but it's not necessary. Just keep in an airtight container and use within about 3 weeks.

Nut Milk

Makes 1 quart (945 ml)

Even if you do nothing else the entire day, making your own nut milk feels incredibly productive and accomplished. It is SO much cheaper than buying it in stores and doesn't have any funny gums or additives. You'll be amazed at both how easy it is and how delicious!

1 cup (140 g) nuts, such as almonds or cashews (or a mix of both)
Himalayan pink salt
1 or 2 pitted, dried Medjool dates (optional)

Grain Guide

Want a no-fail rice-cooking method? Sick of al dente rice and burnt, black bottoms in all your pans? Rinse your rice well in a sieve under cold running water until the water runs clear, and then cook it like pasta in salted water, draining when it's done. You'll still have to taste to check the doneness, but this technique takes the guesswork out of cooking grains. Plus, you can make a really big batch very easily and freeze some for later, if that's your thing. (If you really make A LOT of rice and have the cabinet space, I suggest investing in a rice cooker.)

BROWN RICE

Rinse and then boil in salted water for 30 minutes. Drain, return to the pot, and cover for 10 minutes. Fluff and serve.

BLACK RICE

Rinse and then boil in salted water for 20 minutes. Drain, return to the pot, and cover for 10 minutes. Fluff and serve.

HULLED BARLEY

Rinse and add to a cold pot filled with salted water. Bring to a boil and cook 30 to 40 minutes. Serve.

ISRAELI/PEARL COUSCOUS

Bring 1¼ cups (295 ml) salted water to a boil. Add 1 cup (235 ml) couscous, lower to a simmer, cover, cook until al dente, about 10 minutes. Serve.

SOBA NOODLES

Bring salted water to a boil. Add soba and cook for 4 to 5 minutes. Drain and rinse with cold water, then serve.

FARRO

Rinse and then boil in salted water for 60 minutes (unpearled/whole), 30 minutes (semi-pearled), or 15 minutes (pearled/quick-cooking), depending on which variety you have. You want it al dente. Drain and serve.

QUINOA

Rinse in a fine-mesh sieve under cold water. Bring 2 cups (475 ml) water, 1 cup (180 g) quinoa, and a pinch of salt to a boil. Lower to a simmer, cover, and cook until the water is absorbed and little tails are popping out of the quinoa (you'll see what I mean), which will take 15 to 20 minutes. Fluff and serve.

Soak 1 cup (140 g) nuts in 4 cups (945 ml) water for 8 to 12 hours.

Drain the nuts and add to the blender with 4 cups (945 ml) filtered water and a pinch Himalayan pink salt, plus 1 or 2 dates, if using. Blend until very smooth, 1 to 2 minutes. Pour the mixture through a nut bag and squeeze to get out all the milk. Refrigerate in a sealed container for no more than 5 days. And keep that nut pulp! The internet is filled with suggestions for how to use it up: baked goods, breading, smoothies.

Parsley Oil

Makes ½ cup (120 ml)

A simple way to add a vibrant streak of green color and flavor to any dish.

1 bunch parsley
½ cup (120 ml) extra-virgin olive oil
Kosher salt

Bring a small pot of water to a boil and prepare an ice bath by filling a large bowl with ice water. Remove tough stems from 1 bunch of parsley, and blanch the leaves for a few seconds until they turn bright green. Add to the ice bath. Once cool, squeeze out the excess water using a clean towel and add to a food processor or blender with ½ cup (120 ml) extra-virgin olive oil and a pinch of salt. Puree until smooth.

Roasted Garlic

Makes 2 heads (¼ cup)

Roasting garlic mellows the flavor and gives it more depth. Roast a bunch and keep it in the fridge stored in oil for a week or two. Add it to dressings, sauces, or just smear it onto crusty bread.

2 heads garlic
Extra-virgin olive oil
Kosher salt

Preheat the oven to 425°F (220°C). Peel the outer skins off the garlic gently, leaving the heads intact. Cut the top third off the heads, leaving all of the cloves partially exposed.

Place the heads on a small parchment-lined piece of foil, and then drizzle the garlic with a bit of olive oil, coating the exposed cloves, and season with salt.

Crumple up the foil and parchment to create a loosely sealed packet. Roast the packet in the oven until fragrant and the cloves are super soft and golden brown, about 45 minutes.

Let the garlic cool until you can safely handle it, and then squeeze the cloves out of their skins. Keep wrapped in foil or in an airtight container for up to 5 days in the fridge.

Rose Vinegar

Makes 1½ cups (360 ml)

It's so easy to make this really elegant vinegar. It's beautifully pink and subtly floral—I love what it adds to sauces and vinaigrettes. It also makes a wonderful homemade gift and is delicious in sparkling water.

1½ cups (360 ml) Bragg's apple cider vinegar
¼ cup (5 g) dried rose petals (preferably from Diaspora)

In a tight-fitting jar with a lid, combine 1½ cups (360 ml) vinegar and ¼ cup (5 g) rose petals. Let sit for 4 weeks in a cool, dark place and then strain through a fine-mesh sieve, pressing down on the solids with a rubber spatula to extract the liquid. Transfer to a bottle with a cap or lid. Tightly seal, and it will last a long time.

Seed Crackers

Makes 2 dozen

The perfect cracker. Customize with herbs, or your favorite seasoning. But I like mine plain!

2¼ cups (315 g) sunflower seeds
½ cup (65 g) pumpkin seeds (pepitas)
1 cup (150 g) sesame seeds
⅓ cup (45 g) flax seeds
1 tablespoon poppy seeds
½ teaspoon kosher salt
2 tablespoons psyllium husk powder/flakes

In a large mixing bowl, combine 2¼ cups (315 g) sunflower seeds, ½ cup (65 g) pumpkin seeds, 1 cup (150 g) sesame seeds, ⅓ cup (45 g) flax seeds, 1 tablespoon poppy seeds, ½ teaspoon salt, and 2 tablespoons psyllium husk powder with 2¼ cups (530 ml) water and stir well to combine. Let sit for 15 to 20 minutes, until the mixture has a gel-like consistency.

Preheat the oven to 300°F (150°C). Line 2 rimmed baking sheets with parchment paper. Transfer the "dough" onto the sheets, spreading as thin as possible—you can form individual crackers with either 2 tablespoons "dough" or make a large sheet of cracker. Bake until totally dry and crispy and the seeds are golden brown, 50 to 60 minutes. Keep an eye on your crackers toward the last 10 to 15 minutes of cooking to ensure they do not burn.

Remove the crackers from the oven and let cool. Break them into pieces, if you made a large sheet. Store in an airtight container at room temperature for up to 3 weeks.

Umami Mushroom Stock

Makes about 2 quarts (1.8 liters)

This broth has enough going on to enjoy on its own. Black garlic, an aged garlic easy to find in Asian markets, adds a sweetness and depth that I think is really special. I sometimes call this a fortified dashi because dried shiitakes and black garlic add so much more richness to the broth than a traditional dashi, which is often made by simply cold soaking the edible kelp called kombu. Add a little tofu and wakame and you've got an easy soup, but my favorite way to eat it is in a crispy tofu soup (page 125).

1 head black garlic, halved
2 bunches green onions, trimmed
4-inch (10 cm) piece fresh ginger, peeled and thinly sliced
1 ounce (28 g) dried shiitake mushrooms
1 tablespoon black peppercorns
6-inch (15 cm) piece kombu
¼ cup (2 g) bonito flakes
¼ cup (60 ml) white miso
Kosher salt

To a large pot, add 1 head black garlic, 2 bunches green onions, 4-inch (10 cm) piece ginger, 1 ounce (28 g) dried shiitakes, and 1 tablespoon black peppercorns. Fill with 4 quarts (3.75 liters) water. Bring to a boil, then reduce heat to a simmer, and cook for about 1 hour.

Add 6 inches (15 cm) kombu and ¼ cup (2 g) bonito to the stock and turn off the heat. Let sit for about 5 minutes. Strain through a fine-mesh sieve. Return to a simmer, not a boil. Whisk in ¼ cup (60 ml) miso. Taste for seasoning and add salt, if desired.

Bean Basics

If you have the time to soak and cook your own beans, it is always worth it; the flavor is going to be better. If you don't have time or forget to soak the beans, they will just take longer to cook. And if you don't have time to cook them at all, reaching for a can is always fine! Here is a basic recipe for cooking beans, and some conversions if you'd rather use canned.

1 pound (about 2 cups) dried beans	=	6 cups cooked beans
1 cup dried beans	=	3 cups cooked beans
1 can (15 ounce/425 g) of beans	=	2 cups cooked beans

SOURCE the freshest beans you can—this could mean ordering from Rancho Gordo, or even just shopping at a store you know sells merchandise quickly. The older the beans, the longer they will take to cook, so keep this in mind.

RINSE the beans in several changes of cold water and check for any stones or debris.

TO SOAK OR NOT TO SOAK? I go both ways on this. Without soaking, good-quality fresh beans should cook in about 1 to 3 hours, but this varies greatly. If you have time to soak, black beans, white beans, pinto beans, kidney beans, and garbanzo beans can be soaked from 4 to 8 hours, but sources like Rancho Gordo suggest going no longer than this. What will happen if you don't soak? It will take longer for the beans to cook; that is the only thing I know for certain.

SAUTÉ AROMATICS in the pot with a bit of oil. Onions, shallots, and garlic are a great place to start. Scrap veggies like carrots, celery, and fennel or herb stems are great, as are spices such as chiles, bay leaves, or peppercorns. Add a strip of kombu for seasoning, but also to make the beans easier to digest.

ADD THE BEANS and water to cover by at least 2 inches (5 cm). Bring to a boil for 10 to 15 minutes before lowering to a simmer and covering.

COOK until the beans are tender. The time can vary greatly, but the procedure is always the same! Make sure to add more water if it gets too low in the pan.

STORE cooked beans in their cooking liquid in an airtight container for up to 5 days in the fridge, or freeze for up to 6 months.

● Dressings

● Sauces

....

Avocado Crema

Makes ½ cup (120 ml)

This easy, silky-smooth, flavorful sauce is great on tacos, eggs, and, honestly, just about anything.

2 avocados, halved, pit and skin removed
1 serrano chile, stem removed
1 handful fresh cilantro sprigs
Juice of 1 lime
¼ cup (60 ml) plain unsweetened Greek yogurt, or vegan coconut yogurt
Kosher salt

Add the avocado flesh, ¼ cup (60 ml) yogurt, 1 stemmed serrano, 1 handful cilantro, and juice of 1 lime to a food processor and process until smooth. Season to taste with salt.

Cilantro Chutney

Makes about ½ cup (120 ml)

This is a flavorful and SPICY chutney. Deseed or reduce the chili for a more mild version.

¼ cup (24 g) unsweetened coconut flakes
½ cup (20 g) cilantro leaves with tender stems
2 tablespoons roasted peanuts
1 jalapeño or serrano chili
1-inch (2.5 cm) piece ginger
1 tablespoon peanut oil
½ teaspoon coriander seeds
½ teaspoon cumin seeds

½ teaspoon mustard seeds

In a cast-iron skillet over medium heat, toast ¼ cup (24 g) coconut flakes until golden brown, about 2 minutes. Put into a high-powdered blender along with ½ cup (20 g) cilantro, 2 tablespoons peanuts, 1 chili, and 1 inch (2.5 cm) ginger. Blend a bit until everything is chopped up, then start adding water. Keep adding water until it's smooth (about ¼ cup/60 ml).

Wipe out the pan you used for the coconut, and heat 1 tablespoon peanut oil over medium heat. Add ½ teaspoon coriander, ½ teaspoon cumin, and ½ teaspoon mustard seeds and cook just until they start to sizzle, about 2 minutes. Carefully add to the blender. Pulse until smooth. Add another tablespoon or two of water if necessary. Season with salt.

Miso Tahini Butter

Makes 1 cup (240 ml)

Angelica Kitchen in the East Village used to have a miso tahini spread that was SO addictive. The only thing I could imagine making it any better was the richness of butter, to create something pretty decadent to top quickbread (and corn on the cob).

16 tablespoons (2 sticks/226 g) unsalted butter, room temperature
¼ cup (60 ml) tahini
1 tablespoon white miso paste
2 tablespoons maple syrup
Kosher salt

(Continued)

I like to do this in a stand mixer, just to get it really whipped and smooth. If you don't have one, maybe pop the miso in the microwave for 25 seconds just to soften it a bit so it combines more easily. Mix all ingredients until smooth and combined, and season with salt to taste. Store in an airtight container for about a month.

Pistachio Pesto

Makes about 1 cup (235 ml)

Vibrant green and undeniably delicious, pistachios have a unique flavor that takes pesto to an entirely new dimension.

Kosher salt
3 cups (80 g) packed fresh basil leaves (from 1 very large bunch)
½ cup (70 g) shelled raw pistachios, toasted (see page 33)
¼ cup (15 g) grated Parmesan cheese
1 clove garlic
Squeeze of lemon juice
¼ cup (60 ml) extra-virgin olive oil
Freshly ground black pepper

Preheat your oven to 350°F (175°C).

To keep your pesto bright green, you'll need to blanch your basil, so bring a medium pot of salted water to a boil. Get a big bowl filled with ice water set up near the stove. Once the water is boiling, add 3 cups (80 g) basil and cook for about 15 seconds, just until it is bright, bright green. Immediately transfer to the ice bath.

Let the pistachios cool just a little and then transfer them to a food processor, blender, or mortar and pestle. Give a few pulses or grinds until coarsely chopped. Remove the basil from the ice bath and give it a little squeeze. If there's still some water on it, that's okay! It will keep things moving. Add to the food processor, along with cheese, garlic, lemon juice, and a good pinch of salt. Blend until finely chopped. Drizzle in the olive oil a little bit at a time,

scraping down the sides as necessary. Add a couple of tablespoons of water to thin the texture if desired, and taste again for seasoning. Make a double or triple batch—you'll want to use this pesto on everything.

Rosey Harissa

Makes ¾ cup (175 ml)

This harissa is smoky and gives an intense flavor to salads, stews, and more. Rose, honey, and black garlic make it floral and sweet to balance out the heat.

4 dried chipotle chiles
3 dried arbol chiles
¾ cup (180 ml) neutral oil, such as sunflower or avocado
1 cinnamon stick
1 teaspoon coriander seeds
1 teaspoon cumin seeds
6 cloves garlic
1 tablespoon Rose Vinegar (page 269)
2 cloves black garlic, or 1 tablespoon balsamic vinegar
2 teaspoons honey
2 tablespoons dried rose petals
½ teaspoon kosher salt

Remove the seeds and stems from 4 dried chipotle chiles and 3 dried arbol chiles. In a small saucepan, heat ¾ cup (180 ml) oil over medium-low heat. Add the chiles and 1 cinnamon stick and toast until the chiles are brick red, no longer than 2 minutes—you want to be very careful not to take these too far. Remove from the heat and add the 1 teaspoon coriander, 1 teaspoon cumin, and 6 cloves garlic. Then carefully mix in 1 tablespoon rose vinegar, 2 cloves black garlic, 2 teaspoons honey, and 2 tablespoons dried rose petals, and ½ teaspoon salt. Let sit for at least 30 minutes and up to overnight.

Remove the cinnamon stick and blend until mostly smooth. Store in an airtight container in the fridge for up to 4 months.

Salsa Macha

Makes 2¼ cups (530 ml)

If chile hunting isn't the easiest thing to do where you live, there are amazing online sources for dried chiles, and this recipe offers a lot of flexibility when it comes to adding different varieties. Or don't stress—you can also buy salsa macha online. It's going to be your new favorite thing on just about everything, especially tacos, tostadas, eggs, and avocado toasts.

1½ cups (360 ml) peanut oil
4 cloves garlic
¾ cup (100 g) peanuts
5 ancho chiles
6 Cascabel chiles, or guajillo, morita, or pasilla
2 chipotle chiles
¼ cup (38 g) sesame seeds
1 tablespoon ground coffee
1½ teaspoons kosher salt
2 teaspoons honey (optional)

In a medium saucepan, heat 1½ cups (360 ml) oil over medium heat until shimmering. Thinly slice 4 cloves garlic and add to the pan along with ¾ cup (100 g) peanuts. Fry just until the garlic is light golden, about 5 minutes, then carefully remove the chiles with a spider or strainer and set aside them on a plate.

Remove the stems and seeds from 6 Cascabel and 2 chipotle chiles and set the chiles in the oil for about 20 seconds, until they just start to blister and deepen in color. Turn off the heat. Add ¼ cup (38 g) sesame seeds, 1 tablespoon coffee, and 1½ teaspoons salt. Let everything cool for a few minutes before adding the contents of the pan to a blender or food processor.

Blend until only little pieces of the chiles remain. Then add the peanuts and garlic, give it a few pulses, and you are good to go! Add a little honey for sweetness if desired. Store in the fridge for up to a month. It thickens a bit in the fridge, so leave out at room temperature before serving, or add a little additional oil to loosen.

Spiced Yogurt Sauce

Makes ½ cup (120 ml)

An easy creamy sauce made for dipping!

½ cup (120 ml) plain unsweetened yogurt
1 lemon
½ teaspoon red pepper flakes
3 cloves garlic
Handful fresh cilantro
Kosher salt and freshly ground black pepper

In a small bowl, or the bowl of a food processor (if you already got it dirty to grate the zucchini, why not—but it's not necessary), combine ½ cup (120 ml) plain unsweetened yogurt, zest of 1 lemon, and ½ teaspoon red pepper flakes. Grate 3 cloves garlic with a Microplane, and finely chop 1 handful fresh cilantro, adding both to the yogurt. Stir and then season to taste with salt and pepper.

Spicy Tahini

Makes ¾ cup (175 ml)

When you combine tahini and the cilantro hot sauce zhoug, it becomes one creamy/spicy/zesty condiment you'll want to put on everything.

½ cup (120 ml) tahini
1 bunch fresh cilantro, thick stems removed
1 jalapeño chile
Juice of 1 lemon
Kosher salt

Add all ingredients to a food processor with 4 tablespoons water and process until smooth, adding a bit more water to achieve your desired consistency. Season to taste with salt.

Building a Bowl

Can't find the ingredients for one of the bowl recipes on pages 126-133, or have something else on hand? Use this guide to start building your own bowl combinations. You need to start with a base, and finish a sauce to tie it all together — but get creative with different elements for crunch and texture or healthy proteins!

ROASTED OR STEAMED STARCHY VEG

Winter Squash • Sweet Potato
Potatoes • Carrots
Parsnips • Cauliflower
Beets • Eggplant

PROTEINS

Tofu • Beans or Lentils
Chicken • Fish or Shrimp
Tinned Fish • Eggs

BASE

Rice (any kind!) • Farro
Quinoa • Soba Noodles
Rice Noodles
Lettuce or Greens
Zoodles

RAW CRUNCHY VEGGIES

Broccoli • Cucumbers
Cabbage • Carrots • Kale
Radishes • Romaine
Sugar Snap Peas • Peppers
Tomatoes

FLAVOR BOMBS

Avocado • Roasted Garlic (p. 269)
Citrus Juice or Supremes • Herbs
Sprouts • Feta Cheese
Nutritional Yeast • Nuts or Seeds
Pickles • Chili Crisp (p. 169)
Crispy Leeks (p. 265)
Yogurt/Tzatziki (try the
Fennel Tzatziki on p. 143)

DRESSINGS & SAUCES

Miso Tahini • Spicy Tahini • Nutritional Yeast Tahini Dressing • Spicy Green Goddess
Carrot Ginger • Avocado Crema • Cilantro Chutney • Balsamic Vinaigrette
Source Family Dressing • Perfect Lemon Vinaigrette • Pistachio Pesto • Pistachio Pesto

Gratitude List

SIA, thank you for making such a beautiful world and sharing some of it with me and giving me so much inspiration.

Thank you, Brett, for tending to my bees and my brain and my little fires in the kitchen. You're a channel for a kind of energy I would like to possess, but I'm lucky to have you in my life. And love you so so much, too, Se! Lillian, thank you for everything. I appreciate your downness, and every little bit of hard work.

Linda, I'm sure you'll still be removing cacti from your body when you read this. Thank you for spinning in circles, up down and all around for me, and making everything just a little softer, more beautiful, and cropping just little tighter for me.

Roger (and Mary), working with you was the thing I looked forward to the most during this whole process. I love your work so much, and your energy and attitude and approach to life are so fun to be around. ONE LOVE!

Rob, thank you for exploring the world of cookbooks with me. It's been thrilling to work with someone who isn't part of the "food world." Thank you for the fresh perspective and for peering inside my brain and pulling out exactly what I was looking for and being so, so patient along the way.

Randi, thank you for wrangling my wonky props and wonky energy during this shoot and respecting my inability to mix colors.

Laura, thank you for encouraging me, and trusting me—and for your patience. And for everyone at Abrams for being so excited about this book.

Sarah Smith, I missed you and can't wait to meet the little guy that took you away during the craziness of this project. Thank you for all your support in the beginning and the end!

Molly Wenk, Jason Schreiber, and everyone who helped taste, or taste test a recipe.

Benny Blanco, you're a strange little man and I'm so happy we drove each other crazy this year but made something beautiful together. Thanks for pushing me to be more like you, a person who requires little sleep and only talks about how busy they are. Just kidding, you are playful and kind and my best friend. Love you and thank you.

To Candice Romanelli (Cr_Amics), thank you for all your amazing swirly ceramics, and a huge thank-you to Darren—you guys are the most fun collaborators, and I can't wait to see what else we can make and do together.

Glennis, Hugh, and Ionut— my forever cheerleaders. I love you all so much. You never cease to lift me up and remind me what it's all for and shower me with love and gifts and attention.

Mom and Dad. Thank you, I know I don't have to prove that I can, but thank you for still being there when I fumble. I know I'm far from NY, but there is something in that space that is allowing something new to grow. I'll come home soon. Love you too, Uncle Gary!

To all the Sinclairs and Rosses, thank you for the warmest welcome into this family.

Yasmine Mei and Horace Mann, Lilli Sherman, Darren and Em Mate, Sam Borkson, Jenji Kohan, Karley Scortino, Matty Matheson, Lauryn and Nathan, Dan Stevens, Carla Lalli Music, Carl, Seth, Johnny, Cara

Levine, Skelly + 710 Labs, Micheala and Fred, Ari and Micheal, Andrew and Mara, Lucas and Gracie, Chloe and King, Jess Hundley, Jeff Baena and Aubrey Plaza, Chris Bear and Julia Ziegler-Haynes, Natasha Feldman, Christina Karr, Sera + Dash, and everyone else who has sat around my table this year.

Scott Boggs, thank you for teaching me so much and helping my garden slowly take over the entire property.

Julie and Sebastian Bliss, Isis Aquarian, and Gillian Adamo, thank you for the recipes and stories.

Mondays Ceramics, Block Shop Textiles, SUAY LA, MURMAID, HAY, Le Creuset, East Fork Pottery, Caramelo Tortillas, GRAZA, Upstate, NFS (Jonathan Pessin), SUAY, thank you for sending things my way.

Ben, baby, I love you. Let's have some fun this year. I am expanding with you, there is no doubt about that. Thank you for helping me get out of my own way, and thank you for every single adventure. Thank you for the Men's Program and teaching this only child how to share more than she ever thought possible; life is is fuller because of it. I love what we are making together every day, baby.

Health Nut

Index

Editor: Laura Dozier
Designer: Rob Carmichael, SEEN
Design Manager: Jenice Kim
Managing Editor: Lisa Silverman
Production Manager: Denise LaCongo

Library of Congress Control Number: 2023945803

ISBN: 978-1-4197-7037-1
eISBN: 979-8-88707-123-7

Printed and bound in the United States
10 9 8 7 6 5 4 3 2 1

Abrams books are available at special discounts when
purchased in quantity for premiums and promotions as
well as fundraising or educational use. Special editions
can also be created to specification. For details, contact
specialsales@abramsbooks.com or the address below.

Abrams® is a registered trademark of Harry N.
Abrams, Inc.

ABRAMS The Art of Books
195 Broadway, New York, NY 10007
abramsbooks.com